KU-444-398

BULLYING: WHAT *CAN* PARENTS DO?

Bullying

What Can *Parents Do?*

KEVIN BROWN

MONARCH
Crowborough

Copyright © Kevin Brown 1997
The right of Kevin Brown to be identified
as the author of this work has been asserted by him in
accordance with the Copyright, Designs
and Patents Act 1988

First published 1997

All rights reserved.
No part of this publication may be reproduced or
transmitted in any form or by any means, electronic
or mechanical, including photocopy, recording or any
information storage and retrieval system, without
permission in writing from the publisher.

Unless otherwise indicated, Scripture quotations in this
publication are from the New International Version.
Copyright © 1973, 1978, 1984 by International
Bible Society. Used by permission.
All rights reserved.

British Library Cataloguing Data
A catalogue record for this book is available
from The British Library.

ISBN 1 85424 361 6

Co-published in South Africa with
SCB Publishers
Cornelis Struik House, 80 McKenzie Street
Cape Town 8001, South Africa.
Reg no 04/02203/06

Designed and produced by Bookprint Creative Services
P.O. Box 827, BN21 3YJ, England for
MONARCH PUBLICATIONS
Broadway House, The Broadway
Crowborough, East Sussex, TN6 1HQ.
Printed in Great Britain

CONTENTS

ACKNOWLEDGEMENTS

I am indebted to my family for their love and support. Joan, Eleanor, Seonaid, Charlotte, Ruari and Edmund have all had their own struggles with bullying relationships, as have I. That we have survived so well is testament to our commitment to each other, but most of all to the strength and courage of Joan whose love has borne us through all adversity.

I wish to thank Canon Crosfield for his advice and permission to use some of the ideas he shared in his sermons.

I thank the various publishers for their permission to use the extracts quoted.

INTRODUCTION

WHAT'S ALL THIS ABOUT BULLYING?

Let me make a couple of assumptions. You have picked up this book because bullying concerns you. You would like to do something about bullying. If I'm correct, that's great. I thank you for your interest and welcome you to what I hope will be an exciting and worthwhile journey – and a daunting one. But I wonder why you have been attracted by this book now? I presume it has been the word 'bullying'. Of course it might be the word 'parents'. Or the reassurance that you, as a parent, can actually *do* something about bullying.

Let's start with 'bullying'. What do you see when the word 'bullying' is mentioned? What image comes into your mind? For some people it will be a memory or set of memories from their childhood, perhaps when they were bullied. Closing our eyes and thinking of the word 'bullying' may be all that is needed for us to be back there, however many years ago it happened. Alone. Suffering. Again.

'Bullying' is an emotive word and my guess is that any image you have carries with it strong feelings – maybe a whole range of strong feelings. It seems to me that the word 'bullying' also carries within it a number of assumptions, through association, dependent in part upon our experience of and involvement with bullying, but also on images presented through the media – from comic strips in *The Beano* and *The Dandy* through to television soaps such as *Grange Hill* and including documentaries and newspaper articles. Images of bullying are all around us.

Our mental pictures and assumptions associated with bullying may be encapsulated for us in words such as:

big   bad   boys   them   school   other people's children victim.

You may wish to add to this list any of your own words that come to mind. Some of the feelings associated with these pictures may include:

scared   angry   lonely   guilty   confused   sad.

If you reflect on your childhood for a moment, it may be interesting to note what memories you associate with bullying. You may have quite different memories and associations from the words above, but it is likely that you will have both strong images and strong feelings.

Incorporated into the assumptions and feelings there's also a set of messages that may have come across powerfully to all of us when we were children. I'm sure many of us remember from personal experience expressions such as:

'you've got to stand on your own two feet'
'it's just a normal part of growing up'
'boys will be boys'
and so on.

For me, growing up in the 1950s and 60s, while bullying was spoken of as a 'bad thing', there was also another set of messages – such as:

'it's not bullying'
'bullying doesn't happen here'
'you must have brought it on yourself'
'just hit back'
'don't tell tales'.

Or even:

'don't come crying to me'.

There's also another set of messages, or rather injunctions, which perhaps we now endorse as parents:

'stop the bullies'
'beat the bullies'
'bullyproof our school'
'fight it'
'stamp it out'
'stand up against bullying'

I've started by introducing the term 'bullying' and some of the images and expressions we may associate with it. I will return to this shortly, after I have considered the other term in the title of the book – 'parents'.

'Parents' is a pretty emotive word too. It will certainly carry many images and strong feelings and assumptions for you, depending again on your own experience as a child of your parents and perhaps in your role as a parent now. So what do you see when you picture the word 'parents'? Maybe:

*mother   father   care   love   strong   safe   older
wiser   protect   refuge.*

Or perhaps:

*in care   pain   danger   abuse   abandoned   lonely
scared   unloved   ashamed   lost.*

It may be that a number of words, from both sections come to mind. Closing our eyes and imagining our children experiencing some of the bullying that we suffered or that we know other people suffered is for most of us quite terrifying. The burden of responsibility – and guilt – that we may now carry could be overwhelming. What kind of parents are we? How do we compare in our role as mother or father with the parenting we experienced as children? Are we good enough? Can we cope with our children's pain?

It has become a cliché that being a parent is the hardest job in the world. But it is actually very true for many of us. The pay stinks, the conditions are often poor, the hours are extremely long, we're never fully off-shift, and the job cannot realisti-

cally be given up. The best we can do is often far short of what
we believe we should do. We feel failures. Our children's suffering is evidence of our failings. Their emotions affect ours.
Without doubt, emotion is an integral component of the role
of parent.

I've introduced the concept of emotion early in this book
because I see it as a significant part of both the nature of bullying and the resolution strategies I later propose. A second
significant concept, which I will consider at length later, is that
of roles. In 'parents' we have one of the most fundamental and
powerful roles ever created by society. Also powerful in the
collective experience are the roles of 'bully' and 'victim', and
as outlined above there are likely to be many strong emotions
attached to these roles. I believe that powerful roles and powerful emotions are generally interconnected, and I will
develop this idea later too.

During the last decade, bullying has been rediscovered.
Bullying had never really disappeared but had been relegated
in the public realm to an issue of relative unimportance. I
cannot recall the first text on the subject I came across, but it
may have been an article (which I can no longer locate) entitled 'Aggressors and their victims: bullying at school', written
in the early 1980s by Dan Olweus.[1]

Around the same time, 1984, Michele Elliott founded
Kidscape, an organisation geared towards child protection,
including anti-bullying. Several other books on bullying
appeared over the next few years, including in 1989 Tattum
and Lane's well-known *Bullying in Schools*.[2]

That was the start of a renewed awareness of bullying as a
live issue, and the subsequent expansion in anti-bullying
materials and studies of the subject. This is a brief outline of
the expansion and impact of this renewed awareness.

Since 1989 bullying has entered every British school's
agenda, and it must be rare indeed for a school not to have
ready access both to professional advice and one of several
packs of information provided by Government Departments.
In Scotland, for example, the Scottish Office Education

Department funded the post of Anti-Bullying Development Officer (to which Andrew Mellor was seconded for two years: April 1993 to March 1995), and has supplied two packs of materials to all schools, produced by the Scottish Council for Research in Education. In England, Sheffield University's study of bullying led to the Department for Education supplying every English school in 1994 with a resource pack of materials entitled *Bullying – Don't Suffer in Silence*.[3]

Bullying has risen in prominence on an international scale. Whereas Scandinavia may be credited with the first wave of initiatives, from which Anatol Pikas, the Swedish writer well known for his 'Common Concern' method of treating bullying, has received international acclaim, anti-bullying materials are now available throughout the world. For example, the Australian Council for Educational Research promotes an extensive range of literature. Keith Sullivan, Professor of Education at Victoria University in Wellington, New Zealand (and recent holder of a UNICEF Research Scholarship), has assured me that the fact that his scholarship to investigate children's rights focused on bullying demonstrates it is accepted internationally as a live issue.

Many British schools will also have had some in-service training, and most will have adopted some form of written policy on bullying. Many more educational materials have been produced: resource packages which include drama, role plays, discussions, debates, worksheets, videos and novels. I too have contributed to this plethora of materials. In no sense could it be argued that schools are now hiding away from the issue of bullying. The association of bullying and schools – and its corollary, anti-bullying strategies and compulsory education – is effectively established.

So with all this interest among educationalists, so much public concern, so much investment from Government Departments and local authorities, we could reasonably assume we have cracked the bullying problem, and that it is receding in the face of so much wisdom, awareness and concerted effort.

Apparently not. In the media, in schools, in workplaces and other settings, tales of bullying thrive. The media headlines still announce the prevalence of the bullying problem, and do so with full use of reported dramatic incidents. For example, let us consider an article by Maureen McTaggart on bullying, entitled 'Signposts on the road to Hell'.[4]

The article begins with a sensational headline, not uncommon in media discussions of bullying. In this case it is followed by a report that twelve children a year kill themselves because of bullying. This is the usual media format, with a particular illustration to whet our appetite – maybe, 'Boy Jumps 45 Feet to Death out of Despair'. Terrible, yes. Helpful in dealing with a major societal malaise? No.

In media terms bullying is regarded as a 'juicy' or 'sexy' subject. There's money to be made out of it by the media. The public, we are assured, get satisfaction from the shock and horror of it, so bullying continues to be newsworthy. Increasingly, bullying is recognised within workplaces. The Industrial Society and other training organisations sell courses on workplace bullying for large companies, and there is a growing range of literature which addresses this locus of bullying. In short, there's a lot of *investment* in bullying in our society.

I regret that at this juncture I may sound cynical to some readers. However, all I say is in earnest. We have as a society an enormous investment and commitment to bullying, and in saying that I'm not referring solely to the financial benefits that might accrue to the media. The investment is much deeper and broader than simple finances or media interests. I intend to analyse that investment in this book.

I do not pretend to have studied all the materials that have been produced since 1989 on bullying. There have been tons (literally) of them. This indicates the importance of the issue. It also indicates that the problem has yet to be resolved. Part of my contribution through this book is to offer what I consider to be a comprehensive and coherent understanding of the social phenomenon of bullying. The proposals I make towards the end of the book as strategies to address bullying will be integrated into the understanding of this complex issue, and not appended as a collection of handy hints, so it is important for the reader to follow the argument through.

In the course of this book I review the work of a number of other authors. I do believe each contribution on bullying may have merits, even if by no more than raising the profile of bullying as an important social issue. I would be doing many authors a disservice if I didn't acknowledge that contribution. One of the problems, though, that I find with most of these materials is reflected in part by the fact that they have largely been directed at schools – as if there is a common collusion among authors, academics, Government Departments and publishers that bullying is primarily and essentially a school-based issue.

Andrew Mellor, one author already mentioned and whose contribution to the awareness of bullying and the level of anti-bullying activity within Scottish schools has been substantial, is representative of the 'bullying is a children's issue' contingent. In *Which Way Now?*, his final publication as Anti-Bullying Development Officer in Scotland, he stated that:

> Bullying does not start, or stop, at the school gates. It happens in playgrounds, in classrooms, in nurseries, in youth clubs and it happens on the way to or from school. Children may start to bully as soon as they are capable of crawling from their cots and of inflicting damage on each other.[5]

I do not wish to misread Andrew Mellor. He does go on to claim that bullying can continue into adulthood, both in the workplace and at home. But the clear impression he gives is that bullying starts and thrives among children – although this may be an acknowledgement that the funding for anti-bullying work has almost exclusively been directed towards schools, confirming the Government's view that bullying is an infant through to adolescent activity.

Andrew Mellor also indicated that by the end of his secondment he had adopted a more realistic, albeit pessimistic approach to the potential success of school anti-bullying strategies.

> Bullying is not a disease like smallpox which can be eradicated by treating the existing victims and by vaccinating all potential victims. It is part of a system of complex social interactions, each of which is unique and each of which presents new challenges [6]

He pointed to the fact that in Scandinavia – still seen by many to be at the forefront of anti-bullying work – the greatest success was a reduction in bullying incidents of 50%. Such a reduction, he feared, might possibly lead schools to feel sufficiently satisfied that the problem had been adequately tackled and therefore lead to a shift of attention and energy to other problematic areas.

If we are serious about wanting to overcome and resolve our societal investment in bullying, we have to move beyond the superficial to the fundamental, from simplistic to comprehensive and coherent analyses and social strategies, and recognise the enormity and complexity of the issue. Part of the shift I am advocating is to turn our attention *away* from schools as the primary focus (or locus) of bullying.

Schools are, at best, a microcosm of society. Sure, bullying takes place there. How could it not? And sure, it is important to improve what happens in schools. I contend, however, that unless we address the way our wider societal patterns of behaviour are established and reinforced we will end up tinkering on the periphery, reassuring ourselves that we are actually doing something, and satisfied with a (temporary) reduction of 50% of reported school-based bullying incidents. But then subsequently we might find ourselves at risk, through our disappointment that bullying has not in fact been eradicated, of colluding with those viewpoints which suggest that modern education (or modern teachers and teaching methods) fail to deliver the goods or that modern youth is inherently disturbed and delinquent. Or both. These arguments are heard quite frequently.

I believe that parents are actually best placed to undertake the burden of changing society. This book is, then, primarily designed for parents – all parents – who wish to commit themselves to living in a society which does not have bullying as its core.

In my view there are at least four good reasons for parents to take prime responsibility for leading the social change.

1 As mentioned earlier, parents are in an extremely powerful role with respect to their children. How this power is used will be the subject of later discussion.

2 There are considerably more people in the role of parent than there are, for example, in the role of teacher. In many cases teachers are parents themselves.

3 Since bullying is neither exclusively nor (I will argue) even primarily a school-based issue, it seems more appropriate for parents to be the starting point. Children *learn* how to behave, and children are generally with their parents for several years before they enter school.

4 If it is within the home, within the relationships of the family, that bullying is first learnt, then it is within the home that bullying needs to be addressed.

While in early infancy the child makes demands solely to meet physical needs for succour and comfort, demands that have been likened by parents anxious to satisfy and nourish their infant as a form of bullying. The child then develops and appreciates that the world is not centred on him or her. The 'me' becomes 'I' in the world. Instead of seeing the world as having been created solely for their benefit, children become young people, apprentices searching for meaning and place in the already formed world. Children model themselves on their parents, other significant adults, and real or fictional heroes. Later, as adolescents, increasingly their peers provide a greater influence.

The importance of this conception is that, in opposition to the idea that bullying originates in infancy as a 'natural condition', is pervasive among children and can continue into adulthood, I believe it actually thrives among adults and is learnt and copied by children. The adult response to the phys-

ical demands of the infant may be experienced and interpreted as bullying essentially because of the familiarity of
parents with the bullying cycle, a concept I will elaborate on
later, in which being a victim is one of the integral roles.

Bullying is not the only kind of human behaviour or ability
acquired by young children. One of the most fundamental
aspects of a person's development is the emergence of
empathy. Empathy is at the root of our humanity, is central to
an understanding of Christianity, and its importance tran-
scends single issues such as bullying. If anything could be said
to represent the human essence, or to be an innate gift, it is not
our capacity to bully but our ability to empathise.

Unfortunately, an equally powerful aspect of human development is the emergence of fear, the antidote to empathy. I
will consider the central place of both fear and empathy with
regard to anti-bullying work in later chapters, as well as how
human needs and growth and development affect our predisposition to be involved in the bullying cycle.

Parents have an incredibly powerful influence over the
upbringing and learning of their children. While school has an
influence too, it is useful to bear in mind that a child who
attends school regularly will spend no more than 15% of their
waking time in school between their birth and the time they
reach sixteen years of age. I wish to concentrate instead on the
85% factor, a significant proportion of which is spent – particularly in the earlier formative years – in the company of
parents and other family members.

Parents often feel blamed for the failings of their child care,
as manifested in the behaviour of their children. Blame does
not come into the equation for me. I will talk instead of
responsibility, of endeavour, of commitment, of support. All of
these are important. When we undertake the hardest job in
the world, we don't need negative criticism heaped on us.
Often we are sufficiently self-critical as it is. Equally, we
cannot afford to sit back in complacence. Of course we do
well. And of course we could do better. We all have potential
for change. It is in this spirit that this book is written.

I will avoid the sensationalised approach to parenting and bullying. I will no more indulge in 'bully-bashing' than I will 'parent-bashing'. In this respect it is interesting to consider the media attention and treatment given to certain categories of people. People who bully blatantly get a bad press. Unless, of course, they are in positions where they are expected to be a kind of bully, in which case they are exalted. I will consider this issue in the next chapter.

Victims, on the other hand, generally get a good press. In fact, the greater the victimisation the better the press: unless they are to be vilified for not being bullies – 'wimps' up against 'real men', for example. Again, I will look in some detail at this issue later. The essential point at present is that conceptualising bullying in terms of 'goodies' and 'baddies' is very damaging. Apart from anything else it perpetuates the problem, and encourages 'clever' bullying and dramatic victims – and even bullies dressed up as victims, as I will show in later chapters. 'Goodies' and 'baddies' is also a very damaging way of conceptualising parenting. And for the same reasons.

This book is much more than a 'what to do if your child is being bullied' handbook. It is more than a breakdown of the factors influencing people to become bullies or victims. Although you will hopefully find all these aspects covered too, it is truly a book indicating what parents – all parents – do to create and sustain the bullying cycle; and what they (or rather we) can do to address our parenting relationships and break out of these destructive patterns.

Once we have addressed our own behaviours, within the home and within schools, we can consider working more widely in the community. I am aware of some work being undertaken on bullying within the wider community. One writer, Dr Brendan Byrne, has described his work in Ireland in raising awareness and commitment from groups and individuals within the community to 'stand up against' bullying.[7] My own work in the Edinburgh area with parents' groups has led to one group attempting to help others to form a network of concerned parents who can come together, both to offer each other support to address their own beliefs and behaviours, and to recognise and use their power to change society.

I am, then, embarking with you on a journey which will not just lead to a modified form of parenting or a greater awareness of bullying but to a fundamentally changed approach to society. I am convinced that we need to find a whole, fundamentally new approach, one that addresses our beliefs and attitudes, our thoughts, our feelings and our actions – every part of our humanity in fact. Let us not underestimate the enormity of the challenge we face. As an individual parent or citizen I fear I cannot change anything on my own. But the question I must ask, deep within myself, is: will I allow my fear to paralyse me from attempting to change?

Each of us can and does make minuscule contributions to the way the world is. The world is the sum of our relationships, and we choose therefore what kind of world we want. But you and I, along with many others who may wish to join with us, can multiply our minuscule contributions and begin to move mountains. And a mountain is exactly what we have in front of us.

Even then we need support, greater than our combined intellectual, emotional, physical and material forces. We need to reinforce our struggles with spiritual guidance and support, with a vision of how the world could be. Canon Philip Crosfield, of whom I will speak later, has reminded me of the verse from St John's Gospel: 'Without me you can do nothing' (Jn 15:5).

Each chapter of this book follows the same format. After the text, which looks at a particular aspect of bullying, I include some exercises for you to undertake to help you make sense of the issues in your own life – as an individual, partner, Christian, parent, teacher and member of society. I then include some case examples for you to work on. I use the same case examples at the end of each chapter, so that the learning you have acquired from the text can be introduced into a case with which you already have some familiarity. The three case examples appear at the end of Chapter 1.

I am writing this book for parents, for teachers, for church leaders, for politicians and for academics; and for the benefit of this and future generations of children. I would like to think that everyone included in these categories of people will gain from this book, and that it will inspire them to come together to form new relationships. But I would be dishonest if I claimed that it was primarily for any of these people that the book was written.

Everything in this book – every sentence, every concept, every exhortation to change, every exercise, every aspiration and vision that may permeate it – I wrote for me. For if this book is not about me but about other people, it is pious gibberish and should not be published. If it is beyond me to learn from what I have written, then I have no right to ask others to read it. It is for the bully in me and the victim in me, so that I need not be that way any more. It is to help me develop and grow as a person, to help me allow God to love me, to help me find support so that I can love others. That is why I can truly ask you to travel with me and learn with me, in faith with thanksgiving.

CHAPTER 1

WHAT EXACTLY IS BULLYING?

Given the apparently universal agreement that bullying is a 'bad thing' and that 'something should be done about it', we could be forgiven for assuming that there is a common understanding of what bullying actually is. However, my work with professionals from primary, secondary and special schools, social services, community education, educational psychologists, educational welfare officers, police and other agencies (and of course parents) indicates that a common conception of bullying may be far from the reality.

Indeed, although an industry has grown up around the subject of bullying, as indicated in the Introduction, it has been less successful in meeting our need for a coherent consensus on the term itself by providing definitions of bullying. Many definitions exist, and most of these have been based around behaviours, where the act itself is of prime importance. A simple example might be: 'Bullying is an act of violence or aggression perpetrated by one person or a group of people on another.'

Is this definition good enough? Or does it lead, on the one hand, to a demand for another definition – that of violence and aggression? On the other hand does it not beg questions such as whether bullying can include non-violent actions, or be perpetrated by organisations and institutions rather than individuals? Of course the question of intent, whether through a conscious wilful act or through wilful failure to consider the consequences of an action or inaction, remains unasked and unanswered.

There are major problems with definitions like this, and one of these is that certain aspects of the way we relate to each other might well be deemed acceptable in as much as they are, by definition, not examples of bullying. That is, we can collude with unhelpful and hurtful patterns of relationships because we have *defined them out* of bullying.

The consequence might be that although we don't like particular ways in which people treat us, we assume that we are somehow better off because at least we aren't being bullied. We acquiesce to the ways we are treated, and perhaps we blame ourselves for not being able to cope with them. Unfortunately it is the very aspect of our understanding of bullying that has helped to create and perpetuate many of the problems we now face as we attempt to counteract bullying.

Let me now give you a personal example to illustrate what I mean. I'll mark some signposts as I relate this account, to which I will return to elaborate and discuss later in this chapter.

I had a friend when I was at school. I shall call him Daniel. Daniel was a good friend, we spent a lot of time together both at school and during the holidays. We knew each other well. However, because I liked and respected Daniel I felt exposed to being hurt by him. Point 1.

Daniel had another friend whom he only saw at school. I will call this other boy Martin. Sometimes Daniel and Martin would chatter together and when they saw me coming would turn away from me, or stop talking and wait until I had gone past. I felt humiliated, unwanted, unvalued. Point 2.

In my early years in secondary school I generally obtained higher academic marks than Daniel. I also had a tendency to express my views on subjects. On the occasions I was with Daniel and some other friends, Daniel began to respond to some of my views by slightly turning his head to one side and half-raising his right eyebrow. A small smile could be detected on his lips. He said nothing. I interpreted this as a sign to others about me that I was talking rubbish, and I reacted by trying to emphasise my point, exaggerating it and defending my position more vigorously and intently. At times I gabbled gibberish. Not only did I do this in my verbal presentations but it crept into my written work in class. My confidence in my knowledge and opinions was damaged, and my work deteriorated. Point 3.

I had no conception that Daniel was bullying me. It would not have crossed my mind that that was what he was doing. I felt unable to tell anyone for fear of being ridiculed. What's more, even modern enlightened teachers attending my *Bully No More!* courses and who advocate anti-bullying policies in their schools, which include the encouragement of children to tell if they experience bullying, give me a wry laugh when I ask them how they would respond if I was a child now and told them I was being bullied. What indeed would any teacher or parent say to the boy who plucked up courage to inform them that his friend was bullying him by slightly turning his head, half-raising his right eyebrow, his lips bearing the trace of a small smile, every time he expressed an opinion? Point 4.

Years later, after leaving school with poor results, I just managed to get a place at a further education college. I had moved away from my home area. A week or so into my course I felt exhilarated and liberated when a lecturer at the college asked my opinion – as if what I had to say was actually important. I felt a burden had been lifted from me. Point 5.

So was I bullied by Daniel?

Let's look first at his actions. A slight turn of the head. Is this a bullying action? Half-raising an eyebrow. Is this a bullying action? A small smile on the lips. Is this a bullying action?

If we are determined to separate actions into categories of bullying and non-bullying it seems to me that we immediately run into serious difficulties. Or perhaps you believe we could definitely include some actions as bullying?

What about murder? Probably.

Rape? Perhaps.

Hitting? Hmmm ... ?

Kicking? Well ... ?

When we speak about murder and rape it is usually not in the context of bullying. Yet they might well fall into the definition I introduced earlier. So why wouldn't they be examples of bullying? Some might say these are more extreme than bullying, the presumption being that bullying is less dramatic and less damaging or deadly as murder or rape.

What about hitting and kicking? These are often put forward as examples of bullying actions. But can they automatically be incorporated in the bullying category? It is not a practice confined to Scotland, I am sure, but I have observed a significant number of local adolescents physically assaulting each other – hitting and kicking – as an integral part of what can best be termed a courting ritual. The adolescents, of either sex, who are the most likely recipients of these aggressive physical attentions are those to whom the 'perpetrators' feel most attracted. Can physical violence and aggression be accepted as an expression of love and affection? Or is it bullying?

Perhaps it is more helpful to analyse the action – transaction may be a better word – to establish its meaning, both for the transmitter and the receiver, before we decide what does and does not constitute bullying. That is, we need to have a more useful set of criteria for determining whether any action constitutes bullying than a list of behaviours out of context. An action may appear aggressive and violent and not be bullying. Likewise an action may appear non-aggressive and non-violent but still be a very destructive form of bullying.

Context and meaning are to be our starting points. So what criteria do we need? Let's go back to the tale of me and my school friend Daniel, and pick up the points I marked out.

Point 1: We knew each other well. I liked and respected Daniel and therefore felt exposed to the potential hurt he could inflict.

This is a fundamental aspect of bullying in my experience, and one that is sorely neglected by most other writers on the subject. If we are not amenable to being hurt by someone we do not experience bullying. That is not to say we should therefore become extremely thick-skinned or unwilling to relate to anyone else. What it does mean, though, is that it is essentially through our relationships that we are exposed to the potential to suffer bullying. For us to be bullied by someone to whom we had no affiliation would require them to inflict a drastic assault on our person.

My work with young people has consistently discovered that the people most likely to bully us are those who know us – and mostly those who know us well. We have probably been close friends of theirs. Maybe we are still close friends. They know us well enough to know what hurts us; they know our vulnerabilities.

My work with adults, such as couples in relationships, uncovers exactly the same patterns of relationships. A particular couple know each other so well they can inflict much hurt. An outsider may find the examples of their injuries relatively inconsequential, but the impact the specific words or actions have had on the different parties is clearly fundamental. Perhaps one person failed to respond adequately or quickly enough to the latter – deliberately. Which brings me onto the next point.

Point 2: I felt humiliated, unvalued, unwanted.

Interestingly, the most commonly expressed need from young people in terms of the range of bullying actions is *not to be left out*. The fear of exclusion is prevalent throughout primary, secondary and special education. It has been ascribed by some authors (eg, Besag, Train) that this is more typically the concern of girls. But my experience suggests boys are equally preoccupied with being included and accepted. Many of their actions (including bullying) are specifically geared towards ensuring acceptance within a group. Erikson's eight ages of man, to which I refer in detail later, include the adolescent stage of identity versus role confusion, where the young person searches for a sense of self, of identity.[8]

No wonder young people seek 'badges' and 'uniforms' to show that they belong. Nor do I see a significant diminution of this need among adults. We need to know we are valued and wanted, needed and loved. 'Please don't leave me out, please don't forget me.' Indeed, our very motivation to bear children may be connected with our need to ensure we have people who love us (a point I will address in a later chapter).

It is therefore interesting and not insignificant that the two most common forms of bullying are to ignore or exclude others, or to ridicule and 'slag' them, to separate them off from the 'normal', the 'in-crowd'.

How many marital relationships have floundered because one (or usually both) of the parties have felt unwanted, ignored and excluded emotionally by the other? Although it is less usual for these patterns of behaviour between couples to be defined as bullying, I find it hard to view their marital relationships outside the wider context of relationships. I will return to this link in later chapters.

Point 3: I lost my confidence in myself.

The fundamental intention of bullying is for a person to damage another person's self-esteem, thereby reducing the latter's sense of personal power and consequently the ability to pose a threat. It is irrelevant, therefore, what action transpired. It is the intention, based on a knowledge of the person chosen to be bullied, to harm that person's self-esteem that is critical. In that sense, I may concur more with Besag's suggestion that bullying is more of an attitude than an act (although her definition of bullying focuses on acts). Low self-esteem contaminates many areas and aspects of a person's life, not just the one in which the bullying has taken place.

Point 4: I didn't believe it was bullying because there were only small and subtle actions. I felt unable to tell anyone for fear of further ridicule.

It is hard for anyone to tell that they have lost their self-confidence if the cause of that loss appears 'silly'. How often do we face further ridicule for 'failing' to cope with a deliberate but subtle blow to our self-esteem? Should I have spoken to my teachers and told them what Daniel was doing? Would their response have boosted my self-esteem, because I was taken seriously, or would my battered self-esteem have taken another knock, my ego receiving further confirmation that I was indeed foolish, useless, idiotic, weak and so on?

Undoubtedly, most adult responses to a child's account of being bullied is to ask what happened, to ascertain exactly what action or actions took place, 'to get to the bottom of it'. Implicitly or explicitly a judgement is made. Was it that important? Did he or she get hurt? Are there any bruises? Is there any punishment possible for the infringement? Or is this child just unable to cope with the realities of life? 'Get real, get normal.'

Actions may indeed speak louder than words, in that non-verbal communication accounts for most of the information we convey to the world about ourselves. But there are two other corollaries.

One: it is a blatant falsehood that while sticks and stones may break my bones words will never hurt me.

Two: feelings speak loudest of all, inside ourselves, louder than any actions or words. It's a great pity that most of us can never hear anything beyond the actions and the words.

Point 5: I was asked my opinion as if what I had to say was important. I felt a burden lifted from me.

Being taken seriously, being valued and respected, is the most important way to lift the burden of bullying for everyone, whatever part one has played in it. I will return to this point in much greater depth later. For me, having lost my self-confidence and self-esteem, what I experienced soon after I arrived at college was that I was heard, someone cared enough not to judge, condemn or ignore me; or to have preconceptions; or to be too busy. I was listened to and heard. One woman, by the single act of accepting me, helped me to remove my burden.

Unfortunately, it is neither unusual to have to wait years to realise this is what was needed nor to have to remove oneself to another environment. There is, though, damage done in problems not being resolved within the setting and at the time they occur. The legacy of damage done in the past and in a different place may be resonant within many of us still.

I have told you about being a victim. Many of us may have very clear memories of being a victim at some time in our life. But have we been bullies? Have I ever been a bully? What, me? I'm sure I can't remember being a bully. Nothing sticks in my consciousness in the way being a victim does. I wonder why that is? How come we are able to recall every detail of the hurt inflicted on us but none of the hurt we inflict?

Suddenly I have an uncomfortable picture of my sister as a child, walking to Sunday school with me. We've reached the same point, the cut-through from one road to another, the place where I insult her or batter her so that she runs back home and I go on to Sunday school alone. Every week I do this (or to be more accurate have the potential to do this) until she isn't made to come any more. Sunday school is mine, I no longer have to be responsible for her, no longer have to share Sunday school with her. Did I really bully her? What did it cost her?

So what is bullying? The definition I came up with in my earlier work was as follows: I see bullying as the use of power by one or more people intentionally to harm, hurt or adversely affect the rights and needs of another or others. [9] Power seems crucial. Bullying is the use or, to be more precise, the abuse of power. Power can be based on age, physical size, intellect, status, position. So teachers and parents can be considered as prime candidates for bullies because they are older, bigger, possess greater knowledge, have status as adults, and the position of legal authority in their societal roles. They have the necessary power to be bullies. It is how that power is used or abused that determines whether they turn their potential to abuse into actuality.

But power can also be based on a different kind of knowledge, where age, size, intellect and status are irrelevant.

Position may still be important though, as the knowledge I am referring to is personal knowledge of the potential victim.

Is age important in another respect? Do we continue to assume that bullying is an activity almost exclusively confined to people of a certain age and status within the population – namely, school-age children? If so, is this based on evidence of bullying or our beliefs? Or perhaps it is even incorporated, implicitly, into our definition of bullying? Thus it might read implicitly: I see bullying as the use of power by one or more *school-aged children* intentionally to harm, hurt or adversely affect the rights and needs of another *child or children*

Certainly bullying goes on among children. Does it not also go on, in a variety of ways, among adults? After all, unless bullying is an innate or genetic behaviour, like the infant's constantly beseeching demand for succour, it must be learned. So where do children learn it?

The next issue is that of intent. This is a complex area. Intent is undoubtedly important, and often lies at the heart of the matter. Much bullying behaviour is excused as being 'only a joke', which the person on the receiving end misunderstood. Indeed, sometimes the accusation that the 'victim' is humourless and over-sensitive can be more damaging than the original slight, insult or other act of aggression.

As a rule I do not accept the 'it was only a joke' retort for two reasons. First, I believe a joke is only a joke if the person on the receiving end experiences it this way. Secondly, although it is indeed very possible for people to 'play jokes' which are not experienced as funny or innocent, it is clear to me that if the intention was truly not to hurt or upset someone, then two things would happen: a sincere apology would be proffered and the incident would not be repeated.

Moreover, in any transaction it is as much the responsibility of the 'transmitter' as the 'receiver' to ascertain the impact of the transaction. In other words, it is not acceptable to claim ignorance of the effect of a 'joke' – 'I didn't know he or she didn't like it' – because the person on the receiving end never indicated (verbally or non-verbally) that the transaction was hurtful. After all, if power has been used (abused) the person on the receiving end might be considerably inhibited in communicating how hurtful the 'joke' was.

While any of us genuinely may not realise the hurt we inflict at times, we still have a responsibility to find out. *I believe that the acknowledgement of intent and the acceptance of responsibility are prime aspects of progress towards positive relationships.*

This brings me to tell you about an eleven-year-old boy, who was a member of a group of pupils I worked with once. I was, as usual, exploring the kinds of issues which I've covered above when he chirped up and said, 'Well I know exactly what bullying is.' I asked him to enlighten us, which he did. *'Bullying is knowing what hurts someone, and deliberately doing it.'*

I have found it instructive to listen to children, and I do not mean that in a superficial or patronising way. The greatest influence on my work on bullying has been as a direct result of listening to children, and asking them questions that previously I had assumed need not be asked. I will give further examples of significant discoveries later.

My thinking has, then, been interrupted on a number of occasions, including when I listened to this boy's definition of bullying. I believe that the definition offered by this eleven-year-old seems to encapsulate simply the real essence of what bullying is.

Some writers have included within their definitions of bullying the criterion that it is a repeated or persistent act. I don't find that helpful for two reasons.

First, how regularly does an act have to occur for it to be classed as 'repeated' or 'persistent' – once a week, once a month, once a year? Does it have to be repeated by the same person or group of people, as opposed to one-off incidents inflicted by several, unconnected people? Secondly, is there any advantage in denying an act was an incident of bullying because it was not repeated or persistent?

From my experience with young people and adults it is not the fact that an action (or inaction) is repeated that is crucial but the damage done by the act and the possibility that it might be repeated, by that person or someone else. Waiting for, and dreading, a possible repetition is in itself damaging to self-esteem, confidence and personal functioning, and to the human spirit, whether or not a similar incident actually ever occurs again.

Our lost innocence, the awareness that there is potential for the rest of the world to bully us, is an irretrievable consequence of bullying. We see ourselves naked.

Exercises

1. Bullying: What's it to do with me?

I have addressed some of the kinds of actions – or 'transactions' – that might constitute bullying. Keeping in mind the definition of bullying as *'knowing what hurts someone and deliberately doing it'*, what kinds of actions might you consider to be bullying *if they were done to you*? If you find it helpful you may wish to complete the following scale, going from the extremes of obvious and blatant to very subtle bullying.

Obvious

```
- - - - - - - - - - - -
    - - - - - - - - - - -
       - - - - - - - - - - -
          - - - - - - - - - - -
             - - - - - - - - - - -
                - - - - - - - - - - -
                   - - - - - - - - - - -
                      - - - - - - - - - - -
                         - - - - - - - - - - -
                            - - - - - - - - - - -
                               - - - - - - - - - - -
                                  - - - - - - - - - - -
```
                                                    Subtle

Do you consider some of these ways of bullying to be worse than others? If so, what makes them worse? For example:

Is it degree of subtlety?
Is it what hurts you most?
Is it what you imagine would hurt other people most?
Is it what society may see as worse?
Is it something someone could get punished for?
Or anything else?

2. Our bullying society

Verbal threats and aggressive statements, and threatening, aggressive body postures and facial expressions, are everywhere.

As you look around, do you consider that we live in a society full of aggression?

One way of tackling this task is by looking at a range of newspapers. You may wish to do this with your children too. As you examine the newspapers, try and find examples of threatening, aggressive, bullying quotes from politicians, sports stars, business people and anyone else in the news.

You may also find examples of threats and aggression in:

- The way journalists write their reports.
- The pictures that are taken by photographers (and chosen by editors).
- The way comments are expressed in the editorials.

You could collate your investigations into:

- What kind of threat/ aggression?
- Who is threatening?
- Who is being threatened?
- How is it threatening?
- How else could the news report/photograph have been relayed?

It is probably worth taking time to think about (or discuss with your children) what you have found. Do you think that the evidence suggests that we do actually live in a threatening, aggressive and bullying society?

Case Examples

These are, like most examples of bullying, complex cases. There are a number of characters involved each time. These case examples will be used several times as we go through the chapters of the book. They were first used by me in the video production of *Bully No More*![11]

Case 1

A group of Year 7 pupils have begun to settle in at secondary school. Kirsty seems to have become more moody and not so chatty recently. Two of her friends, Laura and Louise, are getting a bit fed up with her. One day, Kirsty tells Laura that Amy, who used to be a friend of Kirsty's, is bullying her. Laura is surprised at this and asks Kirsty what it is that Amy does. Kirsty tells her that Amy gives her sly digs with her elbow when they pass in the corridor, gives her dirty looks when no one else is around, and ignores her at other times.

Laura doesn't know what to make of this, and suspects that Kirsty may be making more of the situation than there really is. Bullying seems a strong word to use as well. Laura decides to talk to Louise, as Louise is now a good friend of Amy's as well. Louise listens to what Laura tells her, but just feels that Kirsty has 'gone a bit weird'. Anyway, Louise feels Amy is much more fun as a friend than Kirsty is these days. Boys like Amy as well, and Ian has just started going out with her.

About ten days later, Kirsty starts crying at break-time when Laura offers her some of her juice. Laura can't get Kirsty to tell her what is upsetting her at first, but then Kirsty begins to say that David, Scott and Ian stare at her without speaking every time she sees them, and then they all laugh together afterwards. Kirsty believes Amy is getting the boys to do this, and she feels she just doesn't want to come to school any more.

Laura doesn't know what to say or do, but then she decides she will stick close by Kirsty and see what happens. For the next two days Kirsty and Laura go around everywhere together and Laura doesn't notice anything at all. The next day Laura has to go to the other end of school during break to give a folder to a teacher, and so she leaves Kirsty with another girl, Jane. As Laura goes along the corridor she suddenly realises that David, Scott and Ian have all stopped and are staring at her. She feels really uncomfortable as she has always got on with them reasonably well before. She carries on past them, and hears them laughing behind her back.

At the end of school that day Laura sees Amy and decides to talk to her about what David, Scott and Ian did. Amy looks at Laura, and then looks away without speaking. Laura then overhears Amy say to Louise that Laura has gone a bit weird. Louise laughs and says she probably caught it from Kirsty. Amy laughs and they both walk off.

Laura goes to find Kirsty, and sees her and Jane leaving school together. Laura wants to talk to Kirsty about the bullying, but Kirsty says that things are much better now and anyway she is going to walk home with Jane. Jane has invited Kirsty back to her house. Kirsty then runs to catch up with Jane, and Laura hears the two of them chatting excitedly together as they walk off.

That night, Laura feels troubled, upset and very lonely. She wonders about speaking to her Mum but makes the mistake of interrupting her Mum in the middle of a phone conversation. With a flea in her ear, Laura goes to her bedroom.

Case 2

Gemma is fed up with her parents fighting and arguing. They never seem to do anything else, and they even end up blaming her for it. At school, Gemma is not doing as well as she did and this is upsetting and worrying her. What's more, she has also noticed that Leanne, who was her friend from primary school days, has started making comments about Gemma getting worse marks than her. Leanne seems to sneer when Gemma gets lower marks in tests, and she now goes around with people who get high marks. Gemma knows that Leanne tells people that she, Gemma, is thick. And Leanne speaks down to her – when she speaks to her at all.

Leanne is heavily built and likes her food. At P.E. one day, Gemma points out to Lisa that Leanne is bulging out of her P.E. kit and they both snigger. Lisa remarks to Shona that Leanne's fat wobbles when she runs round the gym. Gemma also mentions to Maureen that Leanne is always eating and asks her if she's noticed the way Leanne eats her food. Maureen then becomes aware of Leanne's eating habits at lunch-time and tells Karen. Karen says to her boyfriend Stuart that she's pleased she's not as fat as Leanne. Stuart later jokes with John that Leanne eats like a pig and they both make snorting noises. Some others hear them and laugh.

Leanne picks up that people are seeing her as fat and eating like a pig. She becomes unhappy, and ends up eating more than usual as a consequence. She tries to avoid doing things that involve her in taking her clothes off, such as P.E. and swimming. No one seems to know how or why the name-calling and slagging and laughing at Leanne started, but Leanne is increasingly on the receiving end of it.

Leanne misses some days at school. When it comes to a Geography test she gets worse marks than Gemma. Gemma knows this, but pretends she doesn't. She asks Leanne what marks she got. Leanne feels very upset and angry and hits Gemma. Leanne is given a detention and fewer people want to be friends with her. The teasing and slagging of Leanne becomes nastier and more frequent.

Leanne begins to see her parents differently. Both are fat, she decides, and she feels they are to blame for her misery. She takes her anger out on them by being insolent and disobedient. She starts smoking.

Case 3

Mark is a big lad for fourteen years. He gets on reasonably well at school, although he is by no means academically inclined. He is fairly content though, and has a couple of good friends. He tends to be quiet and keep his thoughts and feelings to himself.

Compared to Mark, Philip is a very different boy. He is loud and has a whole group of friends who hang around him. Philip is bright and, even though he is quite small, always seems to have a big influence over other people. Quite a few pupils are a little unsure of Philip and his 'gang' and keep out of their way. It's not that they are frightened, more that they feel a bit intimidated by the brash way that Philip and his friends sweep around the playground and the school.

However, Mark is being met by Philip by the school entrance each morning. Philip's 'gang' hang back out of the way and Mark's pals disappear. Mark is then seen to hand over money to Philip. Nothing is said, and Philip and Mark don't have any other contact. Mark hasn't said anything to anyone about what is happening, but he doesn't seem quite so happy at school. His friends don't mention anything either, so everyone just ignores the situation. After all, if Mark wasn't wanting to give Philip money he wouldn't do it, would he? He is much bigger than Philip so it's not as though anyone's forcing him. He could always ask his pals to stay with him if he wanted. And he could say if there was a problem, or if he was feeling upset.

One day, Mark never turned up for school. By break-time it was clear that some staff had heard something about Mark. His friends and some of his class began to wonder what had happened. By lunch-time the news had reached them that Mark was seriously ill in hospital having taken a major over-dose of tranquillisers. Some of his classmates began to worry about their part in what had taken place. Maybe they shared some responsibility for what had happened to Mark?

One of these classmates was Gareth. He tried to explain to his Dad that night that he felt responsible for Mark trying to commit suicide. His Dad was torn between dismissing Gareth's concerns or believing Gareth was much more involved than he had said. Perhaps Gareth supplied the drugs? Or maybe he was also extorting money from Mark? Smelling a rat, Gareth's Dad decided to question him hard.

Issue 1: What is bullying?

'*Bullying is knowing what hurts someone, and deliberately doing it*'

It is easier to have an understanding of bullying in theory than to be clear about when it is actually taking place in real life. The three case examples may illustrate that point. There may be a number of 'grey areas'.

As an exercise you might like to look through the three cases and identify all the incidents of bullying you believe have taken place. It may be even more helpful if someone else did the exercise as well and you compared notes afterwards. Explain each time why you believe the incidents constitute bullying. If you use a sheet of paper you could lay it out simply like this:

> *Examples*   *Reasons*

CHAPTER 2

WHO GETS INVOLVED IN BULLYING?

It is a common and perhaps comfortable view that bullies and victims are not us.

> When we think of bullies and victims we have a tendency to imagine that they are somehow separate and different from the rest of us. In one sense they are.... Bullies and victims ... should be viewed as children who are born with specific traits that make them more vulnerable to environmental pressures. They need special attention, if the consequences of their natural tendencies are to be managed.[12]

When academics and researchers try and ascertain the causes of human behaviour, the debate ranges from the extremes of genetic determinism to environmental determinism. Alan Train's statement above is the usual compromise position between nature and nurture, and thus a useful starting point for this chapter. However, Train's claims, first that bullies and victims are children, and secondly that they have specific traits (and special needs) due to 'natural tendencies', are not ones I am wholeheartedly prepared to endorse.

My argument begins by addressing the concept of aggression. As I indicated earlier, there is an element of aggression within all of us that may be demonstrated in infancy and early childhood. Some of this aggression has been attributed to the need for survival, and is based around physical needs. We all have innately aggressive potential.

It has also been claimed by prominent advocates of the Women's Movement that all men are potential rapists. Despite the fury and outrage that arose in reaction to this claim, it seems to me that it is absolutely true. I would add, though, that all women are potential rapists too. Through retrospective studies and the willingness of a few individuals and organisations to allow the erstwhile taboo subject to be put on the public agenda, there is now a growing awareness and acceptance that there is a very considerable level of child sexual abuse perpetrated not only by men but by women.

Current statistics for child abuse vary but an average indication is that by the age of sixteen years as many as one in ten boys and one in six girls will have been sexually abused. It is also claimed that these percentages increase significantly in the next two years of a child's life, such that as many as one in two young women will have been abused by the time they are eighteen years old. Someone is committing this abuse. The reality is that it is adults – a great number of adults – and in most cases adults well known to the victims. Parents.

It is also fair to claim that men and women are equally potential murderers, even if in practice the statistics of both abuse and murder suggest that men are the more likely perpetrators. The fact that the majority of us – or at least it is presumed that it is a majority – do not rape, sexually abuse and murder indicates that some factors come into play that inhibit our latent aggression. This appears to be the basis for Train's tenet that bullies are people who are born with excessive aggressive tendencies while victims have excessive passivity, and in both cases these tendencies are insufficiently inhibited by environmental factors.

I will consider a particular case at this point – the case of Thomas Watt Hamilton whose name has become infamous throughout the world for what has become known as the Dunblane Massacre.

On 13 March 1996, a forty-three-year-old man, Thomas

Hamilton, arrived at Dunblane Primary School in Perthshire with four hand guns, entered the school and reached the gymnasium where he deliberately chased and shot dead sixteen young children and their teacher. He wounded seven other classmates and two other staff members. He then killed himself.

What could be gathered about the history of Hamilton's life was thereafter widely publicised. He was labelled 'pervert' and 'madman' and 'monster' (among other terms). What little we know of him includes the fact that he was brought up by his grandparents where he believed his mother was his sister. His actual father had negligible contact with him as an infant and no contact at all after he was eighteen months old.

He was a loner, who ran boys' clubs. These clubs were sports-based, involving physical exercise and rigorous discipline. The boys were often obliged to take part wearing nothing on the top half of their body. It was rumoured that Thomas Hamilton had abused some boys but no charges were ever brought.

Hamilton felt victimised. He had been banned in early adulthood from continuing as a Scout leader due, it seems, to incompetence but also there had been some uneasy feelings and rumours about the way he related to the boys. His attitudes and behaviour seemed to some degree inappropriate. Hamilton had also been refused lets of some local authority premises due to concern about the way he conducted his boys' club activities. It appears the rumours about his voluntary activities had become rife throughout the central belt of Scotland. He complained to a number of people about being victimised, including the Queen, and distributed leaflets proclaiming his innocence.

It would now be hard for acquaintances of Thomas Hamilton to claim he was 'normal'. Yet he survived for many years in the community. He had no history of mental illness, had no criminal record for assaults, and had managed to obtain a gun licence.

Although Hamilton has a unique place in history for the

enormity of his crime, the kind of person he was is by no means unique. A number of people felt that it was Hamilton who had committed the murders before the police named him. But he was not the only one whose name and character was associated with this crime, either before Hamilton was named or subsequently. Indeed, as accounts of the killing spread, there were doubtless people in many areas who pictured someone known to them as the possible perpetrator. Certainly, within my community I was not alone in remarking on the similarities between a local resident and the character of Hamilton.

But how could this be? How could a unique crime potentially bear the hall-mark of so many people? Even more significantly, if this crime could indeed have potentially been committed by so many people, what does that say about us? To me, and I include myself in this, it suggests complicity. We know, more than we may like to acknowledge, the scope within ourselves and our communities for horrific demonstrations of bullying. The issue of complicity is one to which I will return later.

Moreover, the similarities between Hamilton and other potential perpetrators of his crime are not necessarily all confined to men in their forties or fifties. Women and children can have beliefs, thoughts, feelings and actions that have significant comparisons to those of Hamilton. For example, I will later refer to the case of Jon Venables and Bobby Thompson, the two ten-year-old murderers of James Bulger.

Doubtless, Hamilton was seen as a bully; and equally clearly he saw himself as a victim. Meanwhile, there were an indeterminate number of people – us – who were watching and waiting.

However, despite those people who claimed wisdom after the event, it is far-fetched to believe that anyone could have known or predicted the exact nature of events, that a man called Hamilton would one day choose to enter a primary school, seek out a Reception class, and set about attempting to murder all the children and a teacher. And himself. So what had gone wrong? Had Hamilton always had an excessive predisposition to aggression? Had he experienced environmental factors which failed to inhibit his aggression? How was his aggression linked to survival? Or was he self-destructive, exhibiting a kind of aggression which could be interpreted as a demonstration of ultimate passivity?

An alternative theory to that of aggression being geared towards survival is that it is directed towards self-destruction. Many abusers choose not the safe, secret places to inflict their damage but potentially very dangerous, exposed places. Rapes in alleyways just off a busy High Street. Parents abusing a child in places and at times of day when there is a good chance someone will come across them.

Bullying, again in contradiction to the common claims that it is a secret activity, actually takes place most frequently in busy, open areas. School playgrounds are one frequently reported type of location for bullying. The chances of actually being seen bullying seem a significant factor in its incidence.

The adrenalin, experienced as excitement, arising from the potential of being caught is frequently reported by housebreakers too. It is as much the possibility of cheating self-destruction (by surviving) as the imposition of power through aggression that drives them. Material gain is often of small importance, whether gained through theft or extortion.

One of the criteria sometimes used to separate aggressive people from bullies is to define bullies as deriving pleasure from causing pain. This demarcation is debatable. While there is evidence that aggression is inter-connected with increased adrenalin, arousal and excitement, there is also evidence that those who consciously and severely damage other people are actually full of self-loathing.

Self-loathing may be more prevalent than generally understood, and may be at the root of many people's involvement in bullying, whether as a bully or a victim. Those who loathe themselves and bully may be provoking and inviting punishment no less than the victim who may seek to be punished by the bully, a factor that I will highlight later.

An interesting experiment was undertaken in how to promote sports (and similar research has influenced advertising on health issues such as drugs and HIV/AIDS). Young people were invited to select a sport they might like to take up based on photographic images of these sports. Exciting, positive images of a number of outdoor sports were presented, such as skiing, scuba-diving and so on. One negative image was presented, that of rock-climbing, where a person was lying, apparently badly injured, after falling.

By far the most popular sport selected from this collection was rock-climbing. Was this because of the need to overcome life-threatening hazards, to pit ourselves against the elements, against the odds, to become superhuman – the ultimate quest for (and denial of) identity? Or was it because of self-doubt, fear of success, self-loathing, the urge to self-destruct?

The links between theories of aggression and passivity, and the concepts of bullies and victims, are intriguing. The definition of bullying I adopted in the previous chapter (p. 31) does not discriminate between aggression and bullying. What it incorporates is any use of power, whether an action (or inaction), which intends to cause harm or hurt to another. As the details of my experiences illustrated in that chapter, it does not presume an overtly physical demonstration of aggression, in the mould of a bigger, stronger person physically intimidating or assaulting a physically weaker one. That kind of bullying is, in my experience, not particularly common anyway.

Another presumption is that boys bully more than girls, which would no doubt then be the basis for an argument in favour of girls attending single-sex schools. However, there is no indication that the incidence of bullying in such single-sex schools is significantly less. The nature of the bullying may differ between boys and girls, particularly in earlier years. For example, boys may be more physical and girls more verbal. But both boys and girls use exclusion as the ultimate form of bullying.

My understanding of bullying does not presume that in the process of inflicting harm on others there is no harm done to the perpetrator as well. I am even open to the claims of some who have bullied that, to lift a well-worn expression ascribed to parents inflicting punishment, 'it hurt me more than it did you'. The truth of this claim may become more apparent as I develop my argument .

In assessing the number of people involved in bullying, consideration needs to be given to the role of aggression and passivity within society generally. We do, it seems, all have the innate ability to be aggressive. We also have the ability to be passive. The classic studies of this passivity have referred to the phenomenon of people who are not specifically victims but those – sometimes labelled 'bystanders' – who literally stand by and watch other people being killed or dealt extraordinary violence.

Nazi Germany threw up many examples of this passivity. Pastor Martin Niemöller referred to the ability of whole communities to 'stand by' and allow their members to be slaughtered. The following text is well known in a popular version.

> When Hitler attacked the Jews, I was not a Jew.
> Therefore, I was not concerned.
> When Hitler attacked the Catholics, I was not a Catholic.
> Therefore, I was not concerned.
> When Hitler attacked the Unions and Industrialists, I was not a member of the Unions.
> Therefore, I was not concerned.
> Then Hitler attacked me and the Protestant Church – and there was nobody left to be concerned. [13]

Niemöller wrote the above during a period of guilt and repentance for his inaction, for he considered that he too had not spoken out enough for his fellow Germans. [14]

I will refer to the concept of 'watcher' and bystander again later. First, though, I am concerned that we gain a full appreciation of the extent to which we are all involved in bullying. Experts differ in their estimates of how many people are involved. For example, the figure of 6% has been postulated as an estimate of the percentage of children who bully, whereas others suggest one in five are involved as bullies or victims. A more common statistical average from school studies reports 25–30% of children stating that they have been bullied. There is a smaller figure accepting their role as bullies.

Bullying is seen generally as involving two categories of people, the 'bully' and the 'victim'. Whereas there may be a stereotypical perception of people who may be in each of these categories, Besag (among others) has referred to the interchangeability of some bullies and victims.[15] That is, a person can be both a bully and a victim depending on the social context. This contradicts Train's claim, quoted at the beginning of this chapter, that some children have natural tendencies either towards excessive aggression or excessive passivity.

Energy has been expended on characterising the kinds of people who may fall into the two categories. For instance, bullies have been ascribed the following traits:

- excessive aggression
- desire for power and dominance
- alienation from society
- belief that bullying is justifiable and deserved
- lack of empathy with their victims
- abdication of responsibility for their actions
- self-obsession.

Meanwhile victims are viewed as having the following characteristics:

- high levels of anxiety or insecurity
- quiet demeanour, sensitivity, timidity
- poor self-esteem
- lack of self-confidence
- tendency to be loners

What I find is that these factors are generally shared between those perceived as bullies or victims. That is, people who bully are likely to feel lonely and friendless, lack self-confidence, suffer from poor self-esteem, and have anxieties about whether they are liked or likeable, as well as whether they will be 'found out'. Also they are often regarded (and perceive themselves) as cowardly.

Those who may be victims can abdicate responsibility for their actions, lack empathy, be self-obsessed, be alienated from society, believe bullying is justifiable and deserved – *and* be seeking power and dominance. Thomas Hamilton seems to have incorporated most of these characteristics. I will again refer to this intriguing last point in Chapter 4.

The similarities between people when they bully and people when they are victims are quite striking in my experience, and I will illustrate this further in the next chapter when I address the issue of feelings. However, the characteristic features of bullies and victims detailed above no doubt pertain to a large percentage of the population at some time in their lives.

Certainly childhood and adolescence would be a time when we experience confusion over beliefs and feel full of self-doubt. Does this change as we get older? Do we not still struggle to retain our self-confidence and self-esteem? Do we not allow ourselves to feel a victim of life at times, or seek power and dominance over those around us, to gain some sense that we *matter* in the world?

So are bullies and victims other people? Or are they us too?

Before I consider these issues further, I want to move away from the focus on bullies and victims and refer to another category, the 'watcher or by-stander' that I mentioned above in the context of passivity.

I am unaware of work other than my own that focuses specifically on young people who witness bullying. Yet the most obvious thing that comes out for me when observing bullying incidents is the impact it has not so much on the primary actors – the bully and victim – but on the 'watchers'. Despite the fact that many 'watchers' may subsequently claim that they were not involved in the incident (in the sense that they were not taking an active part and do not want to be held responsible), it is quite clear that they were affected by it.

Pastor Niemöller's text illustrates that well. Moreover, the significance of their presence is rarely lost on the bully or victim either. Truly, it is right to see the 'watchers' as inextricably involved in bullying.

More recent attempts to address bullying – for instance, Strathclyde Region's *Bullyproofing Our Schools*[16] – have now begun to acknowledge the importance of the 'watchers' in helping to overcome the bullying process.

If we consider the ways in which we have acted – and continue to act – that may constitute being a bully or a victim, and then add to those occasions the times when we witness bullying taking place (or indeed are aware it is happening, even if we did not actually see it), we will have a fair indication of the extent to which we have an involvement in bullying.

As parents we may be very familiar with situations when we learn about bullying among our children – often when they have been bullied. It is at that point that we too become involved. We not only have some knowledge of what may be happening, we may also have become emotionally involved. The reaction of parents is complex, but is often fundamentally integrated into the bullying cycle. I will elaborate on this in Chapter 4. At present it may suffice that we appreciate that we are involved in our children's bullying – at least as distant 'watchers' – as soon as we know or believe bullying has been taking place.

It seems to be more valid to ask who doesn't get involved in bullying in one way or another, and why, rather than work on the presumption that we can locate some genetically or environmentally determined personality characteristics which account for the supposedly minority behavioural abnormalities of bullies and victims (or 'watchers').

As I mentioned earlier, I made a number of significant discoveries in my early work with pupils in schools. One of these was about the roles of bully, victim and watcher. Pupils quite candidly assured me that not only did they play these roles but that they were often involved in more than one of these roles. Hardly ever have I met a young person who has not acknowledged their involvement in what I have termed 'the bullying cycle'.

Indeed, they could even be in more than one of these roles at any particular point in time. Moreover, they could switch from one role to another very easily and quickly. For example, they could be a victim in one class at school, a bully of their brother or sister out of school, and a watcher of bullying behaviour between their parents. Or they could be in a set of relationship transactions between a small group of friends where they were watching one person bully another, then be a victim as one of the group turned on them, and then a bully as in turn she or he attacked one of the others. I developed an exercise out of this discovery which I called 'walking the triangle', which has proved a very useful and insightful tool to begin to help pupils in class expose and break 'the bullying cycle'.

I am absolutely clear that people bully but are not bullies. That is, there is a difference between what we *do* and what we *are*. We may fulfil the role of bully or victim or watcher, but we are more than any one of these roles. To see people any other way is dehumanising. It also means that we would be unable to build on their potential for change if we consign them (or ourselves) to the status of one or more of the roles that they or we may play.

How we typically respond to people we see in the roles of bully and victim is a fundamental problem, a problem that we need to address seriously if we are to overturn the bullying cycle. I will elaborate on the bullying cycle in later chapters, as well as consider a range of ways of breaking through it. But there is another important area to address first. In the next chapter I will ask readers to consider the emotional impact that our involvement in bullying may have on us, whether we are bullies, victims or watchers.

Exercises

1. Am I a bully?

Starting with yesterday, examine your mental diary. In it, recall exactly how you have acted towards people during the last week. Sift through the details of your transactions with everyone – at home, at work, in the community. Consider all kinds of actions, any of the ways you may have behaved towards others.

How many of these transactions could reasonably come into the category of bullying? Try and be as honest as you can. You may find it helpful to put them into different categories. I used the following sporting terms for a similar exercise which I originally introduced in a previous publication.[17] These terms are 'aces', 'slam dunks' and 'passing shots'.

An *ace* is where you produce a one-off, unexpected, and devastating piece of bullying.

A *slam dunk* is where you compete to get the last bullying word or action, and sink someone resoundingly.

A *passing shot* is part of an opportunistic and persistent bullying strategy to get the dig in literally every time you pass someone.

2. Is my child a bully?

The exercises following Chapter 1 and the one that you have just undertaken could now be completed by your older children. Meanwhile it may be time for you to reflect on whether you consider your own children to be bullies.

Generally we may be more conscious and anxious about our children being victims of bullying. Are we not as concerned about them being bullies? Do we prefer to think of them in a position of power, even if it is abusing power? Or do we as parents find it hard to believe our children could be bullies, because we would struggle with the resultant shame or blame that would reflect on us?

But if bullying is happening, someone has to be doing it. What's more, if we accept that we live in a bullying society – one in which bullying prevails in many social settings and not just among children – then how could it be possible for your child to escape from these influences? You may wish to consider how you feel about the possibility your children being bullies.

This checklist may help you assess your children's bullying tendencies.

- *How do my children relate to their friends?*
  Positively? Co-operatively? Competitively?
  Destructively? Indifferently?
- *How do they refer to their friends when speaking to me or other people?*
  Positively? Co-operatively? Competitively?
  Negatively? Indifferently?
- *How do my children speak and behave towards me?*
  Positively? Co-operatively? Competitively?
  Destructively? Indifferently? Negatively?
- *Are my children able to express their power in positive ways? If so, how?*
- *How confident are my children in themselves?*
- *Are my children able to tell me if they are bullying someone?*

Case Examples

Issue 2 – Is Big Brother (or Sister or anyone else) watching you?

Looking at the three case examples previously cited, pick out the different examples of characters playing the roles of watcher. In what ways were the watchers involved?

    Case 1   *Case 2*   *Case 3*

Compare the different cases. Did the watchers contribute more or less, or in different ways?

If the watchers had not existed, do you think it would have made any difference?

CHAPTER 3

HOW DO WE FEEL ABOUT BULLYING?

Our attention in Chapters 1 and 2 has been on bullying as an act, and the three kinds of involvement I have suggested so far that people have in bullying – as bullies, victims and watchers. I now want to explore the realm of emotions, as I believe this helps us in two ways: first, it enables us to have a more sophisticated understanding of the bullying process; secondly, it takes account of the primacy of feelings in the make-up of human beings.

We may have some assumptions about how people feel about bullying; and I will share with you an exercise I undertake with participants on my *Bully No More!* courses. First, I ask, 'What does bullying feel like?' The common response to this question is for the adults implicitly to adopt the position of victim and articulate what one course participant poignantly described as an 'inventory of negative emotions'. I clarify with them that it is indeed a list of emotions that a victim is assumed to feel. The following list is representative, if not exhaustive, of the responses I am given.

sad   angry   embarrassed   scared   guilty   lonely   trapped worried   ashamed   confused   frustrated   powerless.

These adults – mostly teachers and other professionals in the educational arena – are then asked to identify the feelings that bullies (as opposed to victims) may have. This produces a mixed bag, and again the following list gives a flavour of this.

angry   strong   clever   scared   guilty   confident
happy   big   smart   sad   lonely   powerful.

Sometimes participants fall into two camps: those who feel (perhaps as erstwhile or current victims) angry and punitive towards bullies whom they see as destructive of the innocence and opportunities of other people; and those who identify with the caring, compassionate components of their profession and who wish to uncover reasons for the bullying behaviour (in some instances they feel concerned to rescue the bullies from their bullying, to make them 'better').

The feelings of the third category, which I usually refer to generically as 'watchers', are again a mixed bag. Course participants sometimes find it harder to identify these feelings, partly because they begin to realise the term 'watchers' covers a number of possible roles. I will address this issue in the next chapter. However, a typical list of feelings is as follows:

scared   worried   excited   sad   embarrassed   confused
angry   relieved   guilty   frustrated   amused   powerless.

Before I pick up particular points from the lists of emotions associated with each of these three categories, as relayed to me by adults, I wish to share with you the kinds of responses I obtain from children when I undertake the same exercise. I will lay their lists out in tabular form. I attach no significance to the order of emotions tabulated.

Feelings List – Children's Version

Bully	*Victim*	*Watcher*
angry	sad	scared
lonely	angry	worried
sad	guilty	lonely
scared	embarrassed	angry
trapped	scared	sad
ashamed	lonely	embarrassed

confused	trapped	confused
guilty	worried	ashamed
frustrated	ashamed	trapped
worried	confused	frustrated
embarrassed	frustrated	guilty
excited	excited	excited

| powerful | powerless | powerless |
| (powerless) | (powerful) | (powerful) |

I will now lay out the Adults' Version above in tabular form for comparison.

Feelings List –Adults' Version

Bully	*Victim*	*Watcher*
angry	sad	scared
strong	angry	worried
clever	guilty	excited
happy	scared	sad
confident	lonely	embarrassed
smart	trapped	confused
guilty	worried	angry
sad	ashamed	relieved
lonely	confused	frustrated
scared	frustrated	guilty
big	embarrassed	amused

| powerful | powerless | powerless |

In both tables I have separated the bottom lines (related to power) from the other emotions at present, and I will return to discuss these in the next chapter. I will also exclude specific reference to the inclusion of 'excitement' under all three categories in the Children's Version until later.

However, the extraordinary discovery for me, when I somewhat naively first introduced this exercise to groups of pupils, was that when they are given an opportunity to address the feelings involved in any role in the bullying cycle, they actually identify almost identical sets of emotions. This finding has been repeated constantly with groups of pupils of various ages and in different parts of Britain, indeed with only one exception – a class of primary school children who had been introduced to a somewhat superficial approach to bullying as a 'warm-up' the day prior to my session with them.

So why is it that children and adults come up with different sets of emotions? Why do children see great similarities between the feelings of everyone involved in the bullying cycle, whereas adults see quite fundamental differences between people who adopt different roles?

The explanation appears to lie in two factors.

First, adults tend to tackle the task by thinking primarily of how other people might feel, not how they actually feel themselves. That is, despite the work I have already undertaken with them to help them appreciate the kinds of ways in which they themselves might be involved in the bullying cycle, they distance and detach themselves from the roles (other than sometimes identifying with the victim role).

Secondly, they revert to stereotypical images of bullying, having been brought up on a diet of *The Dandy* and *The Beano* where many of the cartoon characters are caricatures of bullies and victims. The myth prevails of the stereotypical 'school bully', and it would be interesting to pursue what picture this conjures up? Where did the idea of the school bully come from? Is it obligatory to have one – as a totem, or perhaps as a scapegoat?

In other words, adults respond at a level of beliefs (both about the kinds of people who bully, and how they bully, and how they feel about bullying; as well as to a lesser extent about the kinds of feelings victims may have). However, these beliefs are divorced from the emotional reality both for themselves and for others.

Children are more in touch with their own experiences and feelings, and are generally less contaminated by a distorted belief system. They know that they do bully, are bullied and witness bullying; and they know exactly what it feels like when they bully others, and when they watch or witness bullying happen, and when they are victims of bullying. They do not need to resort to stereotypes or divorced, detached conjecture. They tell it how it is and how it feels.

How it *feels* is – with the possible exception of the feeling of 'excitement' – pretty awful, whether their *act* is one of bullying, or being a victim or being a watcher. Indeed, if you cover the headings of the Children's Version above and try to work out whether the feelings listed belong to someone in the category of bully, victim or watcher, it would be impossible to determine which was which. The lesson I learnt from this and which I want to underline for you is that while the actions involved in bullying and the roles may be different, the underlying feelings of all the people involved are very similar.

This seems to me to have profound implications for the way we respond to people involved in the bullying cycle, in exactly the same way that the discovery that we can all play different roles in the bullying cycle (including all three at once) has. Moreover, it allows us to appreciate that being a witness to bullying can affect people as much or more than being either a bully or a victim – a critical factor also in determining support strategies to help people to break out of the bullying cycle.

To be explicit, if we all can (and mostly do) take on all the roles in the bullying cycle at some time or other; and if we all have very similar feelings whichever role in the bullying cycle we happen to be in at any time, then it is crucial that any attempt to transform the kinds of ways in which we relate to each other is firmly based on strategies that take account of that knowledge.

Unfortunately, most approaches to bullying have focused on an understanding of bullying which has (bad) bullies (who therefore need to be stopped, punished or 'treated') and (poor) victims (who therefore need to be stopped, rescued or 'treated'). The watchers are non-existent or ignored. The next chapter will illustrate that it is precisely these kinds of responses which consolidate and perpetuate the bullying cycle.

Exercises

How do you feel?

Who feels worse? The bully, the victim or the spectator? Or rather, when do you feel worse?

It is generally assumed that the victim gets the hardest time and feels worse. But is that always true?

You may wish to consider examples of how you have felt in the past when you have been in each of the three roles identified so far: bully, victim and watcher.

'Watcher' can include knowing about bullying going on, but not actually seeing it or being there at the time. Perhaps the most significant times would be when your children or partner or other family members were being bullied or involved in bullying someone else. How did that feel? Did it make a difference to how you felt if you didn't see the bullying but knew it was happening?

Which have been the worst times for you – in terms of how you felt about what was happening, and felt about yourself?

You may wish to make some notes below of the situations, and how you felt.

Bully   *Victim*   *Spectator*

Case Examples

Issue 3: Who sees the feelings?

Looking at the three case examples, what feelings do you imagine were felt by the different characters? To what extent may those feelings have changed during the process of incidents?

In what ways may it have been more helpful for any of the adults to have responded at the level of feelings?

Identify times when this would have been helpful in each of the three cases.

How could this have been done sensitively and positively?

CHAPTER 4

OUR INVESTMENT IN BULLYING: PERPETUATING THE BULLYING CYCLE

The suggestion that we all contribute significantly to the existence and proliferation of bullying is understandably contentious. Unfortunately, I believe it is a true reflection of many of our relationship patterns and transactions.

So far I have introduced three roles within the bullying cycle: those of bully, victim and watcher. It is not unusual for children (and adults) to claim that, if they are not actually bullying, they are consequently not in any way responsible for any bullying taking place. What's more, if they are a victim, that's certainly not their fault, is it? As far as watching goes, well, they weren't involved, were they? By 'responsible' and 'fault' and 'involved' read 'to blame', a point I will address in detail shortly.

As I have argued already, I see a more intricate involvement and connection between bullies, victims and watchers than a simplistic and abstract 'someone doing something to someone else'. However, I also believe there are other roles being played.

At the end of the last chapter I referred to the popular notion of the 'bad bullies' who need to be 'punished', 'stopped' or 'treated'. So who decides that, first, someone is a bully and, secondly, that this bully needs one of these forms of response? And who is going to deliver the response?

Then there are the 'poor victims' who need to be 'stopped',

'rescued' or 'treated'. Again, I pose the question of who decides to append this label and impose any of these 'solutions'.

There are similar responses to bullying, which again endorse the belief that bullies should be punished and victims rescued, but this time they suggest that someone else should do it. 'It's nothing to do with me'; 'it's not my job to deal with it'; 'I don't know why they let them get away with it'. Or even: 'I'm not getting involved. Let them get on with it, they're both as bad as each other'. These responses are effectively based on indifference.

The three roles I have just illustrated are those of 'the punisher', 'the rescuer' and 'the indifferent'. These three roles are absolutely fundamental to the continuation of the bullying cycle, making as great a contribution to its perpetuation as the roles of bully and victim.

This is the problem with each of these roles. First there is the 'rescuer'. There is a fundamental difference between being helped and being rescued. Despite the fact that the term 'rescuer' is generally conferred with a positive connotation, it requires the person being rescued to be helpless. It is not an empowerment but a creation and continuation of dependency, engendering feelings of uselessness and guilt. Rescuing is based on an act not of compassion but of pity. 'Pity is a giving which sees the giver in some way superior to the recipient.'[18]

Secondly, there is the 'indifferent'. This implies social, emotional and spiritual detachment. I find the notion of non-involvement and disconnectedness alarming. It presents the same images to me as anomie and alienation, but from a presumed position of moral superiority. How do we feel when we are treated with indifference? Worthless? Invisible? Lonely? Humiliated? Being indifferent is denying our humanity.

Robin Jenkins has expressed our interconnectedness beautifully:

'It is no business of mine,' she murmured. 'Why should I become involved?' The answer came in her father's voice.

Years ago, twelve years to be exact when she was pregnant with Sheila, her father had been judge in a sordid murder trial. The verdict had been guilty, and he had had to put on the black cap and sentence the murderer to death. Though living here by the wood, which was in its summer splendour, and though avoiding all newspapers at the time and all the talk about the trial, she had felt a dreadful but inescapable kinship with the poor brute doomed to be hanged; and the child forming in her was condemned to the same relationship.

Afterwards, months later, when she confided in her father, in an apparently facetious but really desperate complaint, he had asked her how she could avoid that kinship since, when passing sentence, he had known the miserable creature in the dock as his brother in God.

Being born therefore, or even conceived, one became involved.[19]

Thirdly, there is the issue of punishment, sometimes misleadingly termed discipline. Punishment can create and reinforce negative self-images and negative behaviour. It can lead to power-based double standards: 'don't bully; but if you do I will bully you harder'.

What's more, 'punishment is not supportive'.[20] Within schools the ultimate punishment – exclusion – is a form of bullying, as mentioned earlier.

Punishment does not encourage self-esteem, but leads to feelings such as resentment, guilt, humiliation, loneliness, fear – not the foundations on which to explore and express feelings, work towards the common good, or give support to others. Punishment also takes away the responsibility from people to resolve issues, the punishment imposed implicitly being the resolution. Yet punishment perpetuates and creates other problems rather than providing resolutions.

When people play the roles of rescuer, indifferent and punisher, the feelings associated with the other roles of the bullying cycle are produced. That is, the roles of rescuer, indifferent and punisher engender the same sets of feelings as those identified in the Children's Version of the Feelings Lists.

These feelings fertilise and reproduce the number of people susceptible to being hooked into one of the roles in the bullying cycle. One of the most damaging feelings is that of guilt. Indeed, 'guilt is one of the most frequently used techniques for controlling others. It succeeds so well because it hits deeply at your self-respect and leaves you feeling inferior into the bargain'.[21]

Punishers are the great protagonists, the righteous guilt-inducers so vital for the bullying cycle to thrive. But:

> Those who lay guilt on you aren't being all that righteous as they'd have you believe. They may want you to think they're purer and superior to you . . . . What's so good and pure about anybody who wants you to feel like dirt?'[22]

People who are passive and aggressive have common fears – of failure, rejection, worthlessness, insecurity, disapproval. Playing the roles in the bullying cycle is a way of conforming, of fitting in with a pervasive set of social relationships. But the bullying cycle feeds these very fears, and hooks those caught up in it even more strongly.

The three roles of rescuer, indifferent and punisher are exceedingly common throughout society – in families, work-places and in schools. In the same way that 'bully' is a role, which is interchangeable with 'victim', so 'rescuer', 'indifferent' and 'punisher' are roles that are interchangeable; they can be and are played by the same people at different times. Let me give you an example of how the bullying cycle can operate in practice. I have chosen an actual incident from a school to illustrate the point.

There are, as always, many characters, but I will restrict them to the following list. Bruce, Gerry, Samantha, Lynsey, Craig and Jeni are pupils in the same class. James Grieg is a Principal Tutor responsible for Guidance. Frances Horn is a Chemistry Teacher.

All the pupils are lining up in the corridor outside class waiting for the bell. Bruce is threatening and physically hurting Gerry ('bully' and 'victim'). The other pupils are all around ('watchers'). Mr Grieg hears a commotion and sees it as his place to sort it out. He has an understanding of what

sorting it out means. On arrival he suspects Bruce is bullying
Gerry and acts accordingly by grabbing Bruce, pulling him
aside and shouting at him, threatening sanctions for misbe-
haviour ('punisher'). Bruce looks down, red-faced, and says
nothing ('victim'). Gerry tells Mr Grieg that he is being unfair
to Bruce, it was just a small disagreement between them
('rescuer'); and Samantha is bold enough to add that Mr Grieg
is always picking on Bruce ('rescuer' of Bruce; 'punisher' of
Mr Grieg). Ms Horn arrives and speaks sharply to Samantha
for her cheek ('punisher'), until Mr Grieg cuts across her and
tells Ms Horn that he is dealing with the situation and that if
she had arrived at class on time maybe none of this would
have happened ('punisher'; Ms Horn now feeling a 'victim').
Bruce speaks up in defence of Ms Horn, telling Mr Grieg that
it wasn't Ms Horn's fault ('rescuer'). Lynsey says it must be
embarrassing for Ms Horn to be spoken to like that in front
of pupils ('rescuer'). Gerry agrees, looking daggers at Mr
Grieg ('punisher'). Craig and Jeni put on exaggerated yawns
and smile at each other. Jeni looks at her watch and sighs
('indifferent'). Ms Horn gives them a severe glance ('punisher'). Mr Grieg feels very misunderstood and vulnerable
('victim'), and mumbles something as he walks off.

And so on. It could still be running yet. I have dubbed the
roles of 'rescuer', 'indifferent' and 'punisher' the RIP syn-
drome. It really is deadly – and dead useless as a way of inter-
vening in bullying situations.

Every one of the above transactions had something in
common. Each person was attempting to feel better at
someone else's expense. Every transaction was initiated from
a position of superiority. The outcome was that no one actually ended up feeling better, which as you will recall was a
feature of the Children's Version of the Feelings Lists.
Everyone potentially bore a grudge, based on feeling misunderstood, slighted, 'put down'. In effect, everyone could leave
that unresolved incident feeling a 'victim'. 'Being put down is
the greatest destroyer. We call put-downs "killer statements",
because they kill trust and self-esteem.'[23]

On the other hand, there is an aspect of our society's culture that implies there's something righteous in being a 'victim'. It carries a sense of righteous indignation to suffer the unjust treatment of a wrong-doer. In much the same way a 'punisher' may also feel righteous, responding to a perceived wrong-doer, meting out justice. The power associated with righteousness within a justice model is often reinforced by the beliefs and values which are the foundation of our legal system.

But the power associated with being righteous can be addictive. There may be a reason for that. If you refer back to the Feelings Lists on pages 56 and 57, I separated off the elements of power from the other emotions experienced. The adults' version was simple:

Feelings List –Adults' Version

Bully	Victim	Watcher
powerful	powerless	powerless

The children's version was more complex:

Feelings List –Children's Version

Bully	Victim	Watcher
powerful	powerless	powerless
(powerless)	(powerful)	(powerful)

I have mentioned before that young people have given me great insights into bullying and the bullying cycle. However, I was at a loss for some time before I could understand why a significant proportion of the pupils in schools with whom I worked either associated the feelings of both power and powerlessness with bullies, victims and watchers, or even in some cases went to the extreme (as I saw it) of reversing the adults' version completely. In this minority of instances, bullies were seen as powerless while victims were powerful. Watchers could be either or both.

My understanding came about quite unexpectedly. There was a particular boy with whom I worked. I will call him Colin. Colin had been referred to me by a secondary school as he was an archetypal victim. He was constantly and extensively bullied, and staff were exasperated in their attempts to protect him. Indeed, a few staff had become tired of constantly rescuing him from situations, many of which appeared to be of his own making, and had begun to feel punitive towards him. 'Hell mend him' was one expression used. Others had become immune, indifferent to what he and others were experiencing. But most still spent a considerable degree of energy on dealing with Colin's victimisation.

Seeing me as an 'expert' on bullying, they challenged me to resolve the problem. I will put in an aside here, as I believe it is relevant. The 'expert' label fills many of us with trepidation. Interestingly it is also connected with the phenomenon of superiority mentioned above. An 'expert' is in a superior position. To feel better about oneself, it becomes attractive to set oneself up (or be set up) over others. It also means scrutiny by and exposure to others who wish to feel better about themselves by putting others down. An 'expert' is the ideal target. It's bullies and victims again.

Having been set up as the 'expert' (and I can picture those staff members who were awaiting my downfall to compensate their own low self-esteem), I met with Colin on a number of occasions, including being with him in the company of others, some of whom were known to bully him. I recognised him as a 'provocative victim', a term coined by Besag (1989) among others. I used my skills, knowledge and experience, drawing upon a number of strategies that I will detail in the next chapter, to address Colin's attachment to the victim role. I worried about him, was vigilant for his safety and well-being. Time after time I tried to rescue him. I became as exasperated with him as the school staff. I began to feel punitive. How dare he resist my best repertoire of confidence-building techniques? How could he fail to appreciate my assertiveness exercises? How come he wouldn't shift from his role?

After several weeks, and controlling my urge to shake him, I confronted him frantically. Why did he sabotage all the work I was doing with him? Why did he keep on provoking others to torment and attack him?

Colin turned on me. Why didn't I leave him alone? I immediately felt aggrieved. After all, I wasn't tormenting and attacking him, was I? 'I'm only trying to help you,' I replied, almost pleading for his understanding and appreciation. Colin insisted he didn't need help. He didn't want to change. I refused to relent. But why not? Then Colin began asking me questions.

'What do people do to me?'

'They bully you.'

'Who does?'

'Your class-mates, in fact other year groups as well. Maybe even teachers. Lots of people. Almost everybody.'

'That's right. Then what happens.'

'Well, some of the teachers come and rescue you.'

'What would happen if I didn't get bullied?'

'What do you mean?'

'Do you think the teachers would bother about me then?'

I didn't reply. Colin persisted.

'And what else happens?'

'What do you mean?'

'Well, what happens to the others, the ones who bully me?'

'Quite often they are excluded. There's three boys excluded just now.'

Colin smiled.

The penny had dropped. Colin was revelling in attention, although much of it was unpleasant and unhealthy for him. He encouraged and provoked attention – negative attention. He was bullied, he was rescued. He had a great deal more attention than any other pupil. He felt noticed. The price of giving up his victim role was anonymity. He did not want to pay that price. Moreover, as a victim he was generally felt to be in the right. He was righteous, in fact. The ones who bullied him were punished, and often severely punished. There is no greater punishment for young people than banishment.

Somehow Colin didn't seem to me to be a victim any more. In fact, I felt concerned that the bullies had been unfairly dealt with. In reality they were more victims than Colin. They were quite needy young people in the main, with low self-esteem. They were easily goaded. Colin goaded them. He hooked them into the bullying cycle of which he was a focal point. He hooked staff too. He even hooked me.

I recategorised Colin. He was not a victim. Or at least not simply or primarily a victim. Maybe there is no such thing as a provocative victim. Colin was a bully, using and manipulating staff (and some fellow pupils) to punish others. *He was a bully dressed up as a victim.* There was one very clear reason why I felt this was the case. *He was the one with the power, and he used it to hurt others.*

Institutionally Colin was given substantial power – as long as he remained a (perceived) victim. If he chose to change, his power would dissolve. The astute children who identified the emotions of bullies, victims and watchers were alert to this phenomenon. Clearly Colin is not alone. Yet the adults seemed to be unaware of this phenomenon. Is it a peculiarity of childhood? Or modern children?

I think not. I believe we as adults are well aware of this phenomenon because we actually play the bully dressed up as a victim a great amount of the time, in subtle ways, within our families, among our friends and in our workplaces; but we are fearful of acknowledging it for what it is. We complain about our unfair deal, how overworked and undervalued we are – what 'they' are doing to us. Yet we subtly look for opportunities to find fault with 'them', to undermine their authority, to ridicule them behind their back, to set them up to fail, to withhold praise and encouragement.

Over many years I have overheard and participated in debates about how staff in the caring and helping professions (teaching, social work, police, etc.) should deal with offenders and their victims. There was a trend, particularly strong in the 1970s, to see offenders as victims – of dysfunctional families, of poverty and deprivation, of inequalities of opportunity, of class, racial or gender oppression, of society. Most of us were victims, one way or the other.

Somehow it felt much more comfortable being a victim.

Ironically, in the game of bullies and victims, anyone who fitted into the category of 'middle aged, middle class, white and male' could be the oppressors, and therefore a potential target of vilification. Which would, ironically, make them victims too.

The great attraction of being a victim is the apparent abdication of responsibility. 'It's not my fault.' Actually the problem boils down to the issue of blame. Blame and responsibility are not the same thing. In fact, they are completely separate. It is the abdication and reallocation of blame that hooks us so strongly into the bullying cycle.

An exercise I undertake with pupils in schools (and which I have incorporated in the resource materials included in the video package *To Bully No More! The Pupil Pack*) is to explore the different reactions to questions about bullying which, on the one hand, imply blame and, on the other, invite responsibility. I will refer to the first part of that exercise just now.

The 'blame' questions are based on: who? when? what? how? why?

In all cases these questions are met with responses along the lines of – 'It wasn't me'; 'I wasn't there'; 'why are you asking me?'; 'it was just a joke'; 'it was him/her/them'; 'you're always picking on me'; and the ubiquitous 'I don't know'.

There is a direct, positive and causal relationship between implications or accusations of blame and the abdication of responsibility. A former colleague of mine, whose duty it was to investigate bullying incidents in his school, claimed it 'was like trying to grab mist'. His investigations crumbled. No one knew anything. The whole issue was shrouded in fog, and hours were wasted getting nowhere.

The culture among staff at the time was that the school had to be seen to be taking bullying seriously, which meant that someone had to be identified, pinned down as the bully, and appropriate sanctions imposed. Anything less might be seen as being 'soft' on the issue. One had to be seen as doing something, to be getting tough, cracking down on bullying. Punishment was the key, as in all 'justice models'.

The outcome, of course, was that sanctions could rarely be imposed as no evidence could be obtained. Meanwhile parents of children experiencing bullying were unhappy because the school had not acted by punishing the alleged offender, and lack of evidence was seen as a cop-out.

On those occasions when pupils were more clearly identified and sanctions imposed, staff feared the consequent wrath of the parents of the alleged bullies, who not infrequently would arrive at the school, sometimes demanding evidence that their children were culpable, or more often claiming that others were at the root of the trouble, or that when their children were victims nothing was done. Their children were being victimised and scapegoated. And so on.

The 'justice model' of dealing with bullying has a woefully disastrous history, and for obvious reasons. As a model it does, of course, share important features with the bullying cycle. It has offenders (bullies) and victims, watchers (witnesses), punishers (prosecutors/judges), and rescuers (defenders). It is a drama.

The bullying cycle is indeed a drama, incorporating the essential features of the Drama Triangle from Transactional Analysis theory. In this model there are Persecutors, Victims and Rescuers. Associated with the Drama Triangle is the concept of the Bystander – who literally stands by when the Drama unfolds. I compare below the Drama Triangle and my bullying cycle (simplified). In each triangle the roles are interchangeable. The fact that it is a drama underlines the movement involved – the roles remain constant but each person is able to take them all on at different times.

However, the expanded bullying cycle has the following roles:

- Bully: the person who knows what hurts someone and deliberately does it.
- Victim: the person the bullying is done to.
- Rescuer: the person who decides what is best for the victim, just imposes the solution, to 'make them better'.

Figure 1. The Bullying Cycle (simplified)

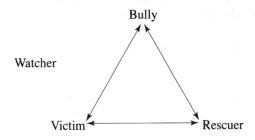

Figure 2. The Drama Triangle

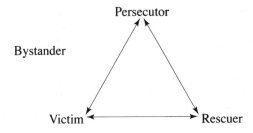

- Indifferent: the person who feels aloof from and uninterested in the bully and victim.
- Punisher: the person who feels they have a legitimate right to bully the bully, to sort the situation out, to impose justice.
- Bystander: (this term is more accurate than 'watcher') – the person who stands by, spectates, does nothing, and lets the bullying cycle continue.

I will now attempt to illustrate how these roles can and do operate in everyday life (see figure 3, overleaf).

There are six basic triangles within this model. There is the original BVR. There is also the BVP, the BRP, the VIP, the RIP and the VIR. A seventh triangle, the PVR, is a mirror of the

Figure 3. The expanded bullying cycle in operation

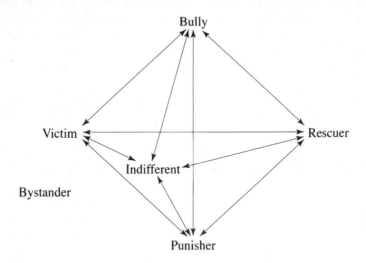

first triangle, and deliberately so. The difference between a bully-type persecutor and a punisher-type persecutor is the moral or societal justification associated with the latter – its righteous basis. In other words, the Punisher is the legitimised Bully. I will address further issues arising from this legitimation later.

Each of the triangles is incomplete. There is a drive to hook in other roles. The BVR seeks the Punisher, who can then seek out the Indifferent. The VIP needs the Rescuer, then the Bully to supplement it further. The RIP craves the Victim and Bully. The VIR will attract the Bully and then the Punisher. And everywhere, everywhere, there is the peripheral Bystander – passively waiting and watching and learning, available for any of the other roles requiring to be filled. Like the spectators at a football match, the Bystanders are as involved in the drama being acted out in front of them as any of the players on the field.

The enormity of the problem to be addressed may now be clearer. As a further indication of the pervasive nature of these dramatic roles, one can listen to the language of popular music and popular fiction. The themes recur. The role of victim: 'I gave you everything and you treated me so badly'; 'how could you do this to me?' And the call by the victim for the rescuer – 'If you don't love me I'll die'. The rescuer replies, – 'I'll love you for ever'; 'I will make you happy'; 'you need me'. Not forgetting the bully: 'You will suffer for leaving me'; 'you'll realise what a mistake you've made and then you'll be sorry'; 'you'll be nothing without me'. And the punisher who sneers, 'Who's sorry now?'

As parents and partners at home, how do we engage with our family? What messages do we send out? What roles do we play and want our partners and children to play?

Of course, however much time we spend at home with our family, none of us is entirely or exclusively communicating with the other members. We are in transactions with a great many people. In each of these transactions there may be opportunities to be hooked in – or to hook others in – to one of the roles in the bullying cycle.

We are unlikely to be aware of it, at least consciously. It may be second nature to us. For in reality the different roles are virtually omnipresent. And we can and do play several roles at the same time. For example, I may be a bully to my son (whom my wife rescues, and to whom my daughter is indifferent); a rescuer to my daughter (who is bullied by her friend); indifferent to my wife (who is bullied by her employer); and a victim to my neighbour. Meanwhile I punish the cat for his disrespect of the furniture (and who is rescued by my son). And so on.

This leads me to another factor, tantalisingly identified earlier, to which I now want to turn. This factor is the emotion of excitement, identified by children in their lists of feelings as an emotion experienced by all those involved in the bullying cycle.

I am aware that adults find it hard to conceptualise the excited victim. Indeed, some adults are uncomfortable generally with the striking similarities between the lists of emotions identified by children for the roles of bully, victim and watcher. However, the whole notion of excitement appears incongruous with the other emotions identified in the Children's Version. It doesn't fit in somehow. Yet it may now seem to be more obvious, having explored the basis of aggression and passivity, and the roles that make up the bullying cycle.

Fear is at the root of many of the emotions and experiences of those who play the roles of the bullying cycle. If self-loathing is, as I argued earlier, a motivating force for aggressive and passive behaviour, fuelled by fear, then the adrenalin surge from the build-up and climax of any incident of bullying – whatever role may be being played at the time – will be felt as excitement.

Therefore it is wrong to ascribe enjoyment, as some do, to the activities of bullies and bystanders. It is in effect the same experience for them as for victims. Among all the other feelings, the experience is also one of excitement emanating from the surge of adrenalin, which is the physical reaction to fear, a fear rooted in insecurity, despair, disapproval, rejection – in self-loathing.

Bullying is truly a world-wide issue. It requires tackling on a world-wide basis. The remaining chapters will explain how the bullying cycle can be broken and new patterns of relationships formed and fostered. I invite parents, as world creators and leaders rather than the elected politicians, to be the spearhead, the example and inspiration (as indeed they are) for the next generation.

The impact parents have on the bullying cycle was brought home dramatically to me at a parents' evening in a school when I was presenting an overview of my work. I had introduced the notion of roles, and illustrated the feelings involved as taken from the Children's Version of the Feelings List. I also examined how this could provide a basis for positively resolving bullying incidents, without recourse to rescuing, being indifferent or punishment. I indicated a range of strategies that helped to achieve this.

One mother interrupted. She stated that she did not agree

with my approach. I asked her to explain why. She told the meeting that her daughter had been bullied by a friend some months ago. Her daughter had been anxious about going to school, was very tearful and her confidence had plummeted. The mother had promised her daughter she would sort it out. She had gone to the school and told the Guidance Teacher to do something about it.

I could feel the distress that the mother still experienced. I asked her whether she could tell us what the school did. She outlined the approach used in the school, along the lines I had recommended. Her daughter had been seen by the Guidance Teacher, she had been able to talk about how she felt, and a number of her friends, including the one who was bullying her, were also seen and told that the girl was unhappy and feeling vulnerable at present. The friends were asked whether they would want to offer some support to the girl, and if so what they felt they could do to help her. It appears that there had been a groundswell of support offered.

The mother was angry about this. I looked puzzled. She explained that it was wrong for her daughter and the friends who were not bullying to be seen; it was the bully who should have been dealt with and punished. As it was it made it seem as if they were all to blame. I tried to assure her that the school would not have been ascribing blame to anyone, but had a policy of encouraging young people to work together, resolve difficulties and take some responsibility for themselves and the culture in the school. But the mother was adamant. This was not taking bullying seriously.

I then asked her how her daughter was now. She replied that her daughter was fine. The bullying had stopped and she was enjoying school and getting on well. 'But that's not the point,' she advised me. 'I don't agree with not punishing the bully and making it seem as if they were all in it together.'

I could have dismissed this mother as being both irrational and insensitive to her daughter's well-being. But I thought about what she was saying. It struck me that the mother was no different from many of us. She had been caught up in the bullying cycle, as rescuer and punisher, and while her daughter and her friends had been helped, no one had spoken to the mother and helped her to cope with her feelings of guilt, anger, sadness, frustration and fear. No one had helped her to move out of the roles of rescuer and punisher.

Yet again I was given an excellent illustration of how the 'watchers' can be as fundamentally affected by bullying – or more so – than the bully or victim. If they are not supported to express and resolve their feelings they will in turn hook others back into the bullying cycle. This mother's daughter was in danger of becoming a victim again, or a bully, or a rescuer of her mother – because the mother was still struggling to cope with the experience of having her daughter bullied. She was stuck. It was not enough for her that it was over, that the situation had been resolved. It left me wondering how often parents, and teachers and friends, are stuck like this. I don't believe this mother is alone.

This mother had fixed views on the nature of bullies and victims, and how they should be treated. Because she was still caught up in the bullying cycle she was disabled from appreciating the full range of emotions that others in that cycle – the bully and the victim – may have.

Exercises

Working on the Bullying Cycle.

What does the diagram (opposite) mean to you in terms of the relationships you have?

Can you see yourself in each these roles, and moving between them?

You may find it useful to spend time reflecting on these roles, and identifying not only the roles you play but also who else is in the various triangles with you.

You may also wish to keep in mind the times you are a Bystander.

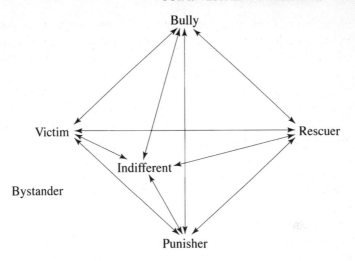

Case Examples

Issue 4: From Feelings to Roles

In the third issue I asked you to consider the feelings that were seen (or not seen), and how a response at the level of feelings might have been constructively undertaken.

Looking again at the case examples, you may wish to identify the more complex roles that I have introduced during this chapter, and clarify which sets of roles and triangles may have been at play at any particular time. It may also be helpful to reflect on the position of bystanders. Do you see them hooked into the bullying cycle at times?

CHAPTER 5

HOW DO WE BREAK THE BULLYING CYCLE?

Given the enormity of the problem, it is reasonable to question whether we really *want* to set about breaking the bullying cycle, before we look at ways in which we may be able to do this. After all, it means breaking with what may well be familiar and comfortable, and fundamental, patterns of behaviour. None of us behaves in a social vacuum. Therefore if one person changes, it affects all (or at least most) of their relationships. This will often lead to tension and confusion, and frequently resistance, among other people in the social networks.

Change is always difficult. The individual can easily be overwhelmed. We have a choice, though, whether to respond positively to the challenge to change or acquiesce and conform to old, familiar and unhealthy patterns of behaviour and relationships. To follow the latter course is to accept impotence. It is to be a victim.

Attempts to change others, to make them behave in ways that meet our expectations, are likely to be 'more of the same' – that is, the change is imposed, and the instigator falls into the role of bully; or the role of punisher, should the person targeted for change not respond in the desired manner.

A good example of this approach is related in Maureen Taggart's article on bullying, referred to earlier.[24] Michelle Elliott of Kidscape, an organisation whose work is described by Taggart as 'the most well-known of all the anti-bullying and general child safety initiatives', is reported as advocating 'whatever means necessary – guilt, shame or even bribery' to tackle a child involved in bullying, followed by strictly imposed rules on behaviour and sanctions for non-compliance.

The Kidscape line, then, is to promote an archetypal bullying response to a bullying incident, first by shaming children and subsequently (through the adoption of tight contracts) by instituting a high probability of failure and the consequent imposition of punishment through exclusion, in effect a further form of bullying.

There is evidence that children assessed as being bullies in primary school are around four times more likely to be bullies and victims in later years. The reason for this is not to do with the fact that bullying has been ignored. I believe it is a direct consequence of the blaming and shaming of these children who have been suspected of bullying. Rather than encourage change, the supposed anti-bullying strategies have confirmed these children's negative self-esteem, fed their feelings of self-loathing, and consolidated their places in the bullying cycle, thus condemning them to a spiral out of which it is hard to break.

However, I believe that change is not about others. It is about us. It is about me. As parents it is neither appropriate nor enough to set about changing our children. If we are serious about wanting the world to be different for them we have to set them the example. We need to examine ourselves. We need to break the bullying cycles of which we are an integral part. Then, by example more than instruction, we can help our children to change.

If change is to take place then each of us has to understand what is involved, and have the skills to implement it. But far more importantly, the individual has to want to change and believe that change is possible. Approaches that focus on cognitive-behavioural approaches, where the 'thinking' and 'doing' levels are the prime focus for change, can appear attractive. Usually there is a clear contract established, and often some progress results fairly quickly. This makes sense, as people can more easily learn new skills and gain knowledge.

Work to raise self-esteem (some of which I will introduce later), has sometimes been based on a cognitive-behavioural approach, such as that undertaken by Michael Bernard in California (and which has proven popular in Australia and New Zealand). Achievement is here seen as the basis of self-esteem. These methods can produce immediately effective results. However, change is usually short-lived. The reason for this is that the long-term scope for change requires that a person addresses their feelings and beliefs. These are remarkably resistant to change, and frequently avoided by those wishing to encourage change in others.

For example, my wife and I had an agreement to share the housework. I understood what housework was, what needed to be done and when, and I had the skills and ability to undertake the tasks. From a cognitive-behavioural point of view, the verbal contract enshrined the necessary 'thinking' and 'doing' levels to effect change. And in the initial period following this agreement, it worked well. We could even reward ourselves for the achievement.

However, older patterns began to re-emerge. This was not resolved by a 'problem-solving' approach, as the problem was neither one of rationality nor of practice. The problem was that I didn't really believe in the agreement, and I didn't feel that doing as much housework was what I wanted to do with my time. I thought it was right, it sounded fair (and I wanted to see myself as a fair person), it fitted into the concept of equality I endorsed, but. . . .

I could (and did) make excuses – rational explanations for my failure to deliver the goods, such as 'I've been too busy'; 'I forgot'; 'I was going to do it later' – but none of my attempts to get back on track worked. Basically I didn't want the agreement. The outcome was, not surprisingly, tension and frustration for both of us, defensiveness from me, and a sense of failure. Rather than resolve the housework issue, it created the solid foundation for the bullying cycle, where points are scored against each other, as both of us were hurting and feeling misused, undervalued and vulnerable. We could have perceived ourselves as victims of the other's bullying.

Schools are generally able to produce an anti-bullying policy. They have an apparent understanding of what bullying is, and a prescribed course or courses of action to respond to incidents. This is usually enshrined in a policy document, in effect a form of contract. The 'thinking' and 'doing' levels are displayed clearly. But commentators often report that schools do not seem to be effective in implementing their explicit policy. Some doubt the schools' commitment to it. Do they really want to do something about bullying? Do they really believe they can?

Of course, reasons and explanations, often from the perspective of a victim who does not want to be deemed to be at fault, are given for any shortfall in delivering the goods – staff shortages or sickness, lack of evidence, insufficient information, communication problems, or the allegation that it was someone else's responsibility. What's more, if parents only did their job right. . . . As if to ensure the removal of any remaining basis for possible accusations of blameworthiness, there is always great activity and busy-ness. However, 'We do not face up to the basic question: *What is the potential for change within educational institutions as presently constituted?* A lot of activity does not necessarily mean action.'[25]

The bottom line, the real problem, is rarely at the level of thinking and doing. The problem will be located in the area of beliefs and emotions. So, therefore, will be the solution.

Any strategies we adopt to tackle bullying within our homes, schools, workplaces and community need to be based on the *belief* that it is possible to break the bullying cycle, that it would allow a more positive society to emerge, that all of us can make a difference, that it is something that is worth us doing; and on the *feeling* that it is something we really want to do, that we have something to offer, that we are worth something better. Otherwise, let's forget it. Posturing, saying the right things, making empty promises – all these are dishonest and detract from and undermine the possibility of social change.

So what can each of us at an individual level actually do? It seems to me that fundamentally we have to get ourselves out of patterns of behaviour that lead to us playing one of the roles in the bullying cycle. We have to stop ourselves being a rescuer, indifferent, punisher and bystander – as well as being a bully and victim. We have to become survivors of the bullying cycle.

Essentially all these roles have the same ingredients. They are based on relationships of inequality, of superiority and inferiority. They are associated with similar sets of emotions. And they are roles that all of us can and do play. Therefore it is not surprising that the way to break the bullying cycle at an individual level is essentially the same for all of us, whichever roles we consider ourselves to play.

I will outline a number of issues to address, as well as strategies and techniques that can help prepare us as individuals. I have collated these under four headings – beliefs, thoughts, feelings and actions – although it is correct to consider that some of the techniques work on more than one level.

1 Beliefs: our values; how we see ourselves and the world.

(a) People are either passive or aggressive

Is it true that there are only two kinds of ways of being, passive or aggressive? Do we want to be passive? Or aggressive? What about the concept of being assertive? Or is that another form of aggression?

This is a fraught area in my experience, and it underlies some of the ambivalent and contradictory responses to bullying. Alan Train, in a recent book aimed at teachers and parents, introduces the subject of bullying by pointing out the tendencies of his audience to avoid facing up to the issue. He explains:

Perhaps the unease experienced by both parents and professionals when they encounter bullying springs from an underlying
ambivalence towards the issue. Although most people have an
innate dislike of bullies, they do admire and envy dominant personalities for the power they hold.[26]

Unfortunately, at this point his logic becomes confusing for
he continues: 'If they had a choice for a child to be either
passive or assertive, most would prefer the latter. . . . it is the
perception of most adults that dominant personalities are
happier people.'[27]

Leaving aside for the moment whether or not parents
and teachers would prefer assertive children, and the
alleged causal correlation between dominance and happi-
ness, the assumption Train is making is that these dominant young people are assertive rather than aggressive; and
that they are essentially likely to be – or to be more accurate, are likely to be perceived to be – admirable, happy
bullies.

The confusion between aggression and assertiveness is
widespread. I was once admonished brusquely by a senior
teacher when I exhorted the merits of assertiveness training
for pupils. Defensively fending off the image presented to him
of confident young people, he advised me: 'We don't want
them being cheeky.'

There is a fundamental difference between passivity and
assertion. There is also a fundamental difference between
aggression and assertion. Moreover, aggression and passivity
are at opposite ends of the same linear continuum, whereas
assertiveness isn't part of that line at all. Aggression is the
attempt or practice of intimidation, the imposition of one
person's will over another, the threat of the potential abuse of
power.

Often the term aggression is used as a positive attribute
when referring to sports. An excellent description of how foot-
ballers use their aggression was given by Italian international
Pasquale Bruno, the Heart of Midlothian defender, in an
interview for the *Daily Record*:

My job is to stop the best player in the other team scoring goals against my team – I do what I have to do. I am not a dirty player, but when I play against a Van Basten or a Careca, I tug their jerseys a little – what else can you do?

I do not have the technical ability of these men. *I do not set out to kick people. But I want them to know that I am capable of it, to make them a little nervous.* [28]

Passivity, at the other extreme, is the abdication of will, the acquiescence to other people's wishes, the denial of self in the face of another's aggression. It is a chosen behaviour. The concept of a totally passive personality is virtually unheard of. No one is passive all the time. People when passive are dominated because they allow it or collude with being treated this way. Victims and bystanders are passive.

Moreover, I earlier stated that the bullying cycle was formed from relationships between people. The reality we have to appreciate is that a person dominating or being aggressive has actually learnt how to inflict this on the passive person from the latter. That is, the victim is as responsible for teaching the aggressor how and when to dominate the victim as the aggressor is in teaching the passive person how and when to be a victim.

The gist of the matter is this: passive people are trained by aggressive people to be passive. However, these same passive people in turn are training the aggressive ones to be more aggressive. One trains the other. They couldn't live without the rewards each gives the other. [29]

I consider the 'rewards' referred to by Hauck as being essentially negative 'pay-offs', notwithstanding the kudos that can be attracted by both bullies and victims in our society. As I have already illustrated, the greater the victimisation the greater the sympathy, and even the monetary or material rewards. Both passivity and aggression are based on unequal relationships. A person who is being aggressive puts others down – such a person is in a one-up role. A person who is being passive is put down – such a person is in a one-down role.

By contrast, a person who is being assertive is expressing their own ideas, wishes, beliefs and talents to fulfil their own abilities and potential, to free their own will – but not at the expense of anyone else. 'I am being assertive when I experience a sense of myself and can hold onto it no matter what I'm feeling. I then respect the same reality in the other person.' [30]

Assertiveness is also the basis for personal growth and change. 'Assertiveness means finding out why I behave the way I do, why I want what I want and then deciding whether this behaviour is really necessary or really me.'[31]

They do not put others down, nor do they allow themselves to be put down. They see other people as having the right to be assertive themselves. They are neither one-up nor one-down with respect to anyone else. People in the roles of bully, rescuer, indifferent, and punisher are being one-up. As such they are *all* being aggressive. The victim is one-down.

However, many adults struggle to accept young people being assertive. Their belief system, whether or not it is explicitly articulated, holds that young people should be in an inferior position. 'Adults know best'; 'respect your elders'; and the classic double-standard: 'do what I say, not what I do'.

Teachers like the senior teacher I quoted above equate the open and honest expression of opinions (assertiveness) with cheek (the ridiculing of teachers' opinions). This is also apparent in the arena of parent-teacher transactions, where there are still many teachers who resent parental equality of opinions on educational matters. Likewise, many parents, particularly those who work outside business management and the professions, still feel put down by teachers (and other professionals), and respond either passively ('teacher knows best') or counter-aggressively ('who do you think you are?'). In much the same way does Pasquale Bruno attempt to put down opposing strikers before they put him down.

The scenario portrayed above can also apply in reverse. Teachers often feel under threat from parents, and parents can be abusive towards teachers and destructive of teachers' authority.

Aggression, counter-aggression and passivity, the battle for superiority and dominance, is all-pervasive. Our society, as Train states, prefers those who are dominant. The problem is, however, that to be dominant someone has to be inferior. Our society requires bullies and victims. Some parents tell their children to hit back (counter-aggression). Some even tell their child to get in first (to bully as a supposed form of pre-emptive counter-aggression) and refuse to countenance tales of bullying (although I am unsure how they respond if their child is then met with counter-aggression). I am less familiar with parents who tell their child to turn the other cheek.

So what do we believe? Is it:

'an eye for an eye'
'forgive your transgressor seventy times seven times'
'crime deserves punishment'
'ignore them and they will go away'
'they must be given help'
'they must be stopped in their tracks'
'show them you mean business and you won't be bullied'?

There are numerous possible beliefs. I have no intention of imposing mine, but I do ask you to consider how your beliefs fit into the bullying cycle. Do they contribute to one or more of the roles there? Or do they contribute to the breaking down of the bullying cycle?

(b) There will always be bullying.

It may be unkind to regard as cynical those who believe bullying cannot be eradicated from society. It is on face value a realistic statement. But if people believe this it will be reflected in their actions. It will be confirmed – as it currently is – as a self-fulfilling prophecy. I am not asking anyone to change their beliefs. I am asking that consideration is given to how beliefs such as this may perpetuate the bullying cycle, and whether therefore there is a desire to change them. After all, it is unrealistic to seek to practise or create something in which you have no faith.

(c) I am not able to change such an enormous social problem.

What disables us? What do we need to be stronger? What faith do we need in ourselves to be able to assert our beliefs and values, and how do we get that faith? There may be a link with how we feel. Do we want to be able and strong enough, or is it too much responsibility? Would we rather someone else sorted it out for us? If so, does that not sound like we are passive and needing someone to rescue us? Is not this belief typically that of the victim in the bullying cycle?

(d) Feelings are 'bad' or 'wrong'.

It is a source of concern and sadness to me to witness how young people are taught in many schools, particularly in the secondary sector. Generally there is a good deal of attention paid to intellectual understanding and practical skills, and schools preen themselves on their academic results and sports, arts and musical achievements. However, these successes are partial as they are undertaken in an emotional desert. Literacy in emotions is not on the curriculum.

There are clear parallels between literacy in language and literacy in emotions. We learn to write and to read what we have written. We learn to read what others have written. We like to play with words ourselves and we encourage others to experiment with language. Increasingly there is less recourse to linguistic convention, and less fear of language. We are more able to express ourselves freely.

Likewise, to be emotionally literate we need to develop the ability to recognise how we feel – to 'read' how we feel – and the ability to communicate it to others. Further, we require the ability to allow others to express how they feel.

The attraction of cognitive-behavioural approaches as mentioned above – for example, for problem-solving – is in part the ease with which they fit into current school curricula. There is little focus on how pupils feel. Moreover, teachers have often expressed their fear of feelings. They may shy away from allowing pupils to talk about their personal experiences

– 'we don't want them getting upset' – or they may contend that discussion of feelings is intrusive, an invasion of privacy.

Why feelings, as opposed to thoughts, should accrue the label of personal and, further, the consequent banishment of them from school life appears irrational (that is, emotional) to me. The image vividly emerges of an impersonal school. Irrational it may well be. Why would we want this? What are we so scared of?

Fear prevails. The fear that if feelings are expressed by one pupil it will encourage others to share theirs, that it might get out of control. Uncontrolled emotions, especially for teachers unsure about their own emotional literacy, are a real threat. Thoughts are much safer. The message passed on through the educational system, then, is that feelings are unimportant and (perhaps) should only be expressed between consenting parties in private. Or better still, kept to yourself. Are feelings somehow 'bad' and 'sordid'? I may feel bad about myself in some way. That doesn't mean that it is bad of me to have feelings.

I consider that feelings are amoral – that is, they are neither good nor bad, they have no moral value as such. They exist. We may need to address our beliefs, to allow ourselves to realise that we all can and do have a full range of feelings, many of which we may deny or repress. It is increasingly accepted that the repression of feelings may induce physical illness.

Women have traditionally been more able (or more permitted) to express feelings; but the cost of this has been the devaluation of their contribution to society. Intuition, based on emotional literacy, has no place in the rational-intellectual world. Perhaps this has been ideally conveyed by the edict 'big boys don't cry'.

2 Thoughts: using our intellect and ability to reason.

(a) The snap-shot

We need to understand what is happening to us and to those around us. Part of this is understanding what roles may be in play at any one time. The first task is, literally, to stop and think. The snap-shot is an attempt to become aware, to see ourselves. In the course of any interaction our beliefs and feelings may be driving our actions. The ability to cut across this interaction, to present ourselves with a still picture of what is happening and why we are behaving in certain ways, is a valuable aid in our attempts to understand (and subsequently break) patterns of behaviour.

This is not an implicit invitation to confront other people with your understanding of their part in the process, such as 'ah-ha, Albert, you're being a victim' or 'oh dear, Lucinda, you're doing a spot of rescuing again'. However, it may be a good opportunity to confront your own actions. I will identify some possibilities shortly.

(b) The process recording.

This is a favourite technique inflicted on social-work students by their practice teachers, but probably never used again after the student has fully entered the professional ranks. The process recording analyses afterwards the transactions that have taken place. So what exactly was happening? Why did we end up arguing about that? What led me to be that way?

The intention is not just to have an account of the dialogue but a full understanding of the other communications that were going on. It is important to be aware of all the non-verbal communication, such as the facial expressions, the eye contact, the hand and leg movements. Some body movements mean more to us than others, because of our history. As you may appreciate, I am particularly sensitive still to movements of eyebrows, with or without supercilious smiles.

Be aware too of the feelings that were experienced by you. How did you convey these in your communications?

(c) The history lesson.

How come it always seems to end up the same way? What patterns do I recognise from every conversation or interaction? For example: 'He arrives home and demands my attention. I ask him to wait and he has a tantrum. I tell him to grow up and he goes off in a sulk until his sister comes home and she then spends hours trying to make him laugh. Then he acts like nothing has happened, asks me what's wrong and tells me I'm always being moody and it's about time I smiled and enjoyed life.'

If the interaction sounds familiar, then work out what roles are being played, who is playing them and when. Some patterns last for decades. For some people there is a lifetime script of being a victim or a bully or a rescuer. Or all of these and more.

(d) The triggers.

What triggers off my reactions? When my button has been pressed and I am on course to explode into aggression or sink into passivity, it may be considerably more useful for me to interrupt my usual responses by working out what has been said or done to provoke this familiar response. The ability to know one's triggers is the first step both to anticipating them (and thereby having an opportunity to break with the normal response – see below under '*actions*'); and to work on dealing with the issues that have produced these triggers (which in many cases may be relics of earlier survival techniques from our childhood, but which have outlived their usefulness, and are no doubt connected with our feelings of self-worth and self-belief – see below).

Listing our trigger points, and gaining some insight into why certain things do trigger off our responses, is crucial in breaking our patterns of unhealthy behaviour.

(e) Passivity, aggression and assertiveness – checking out our codes.

It is vital that we understand the difference between being passive, being aggressive and being assertive, as explained above. It is also vital that we can establish how we are actually being at any one time. We need to know that the way we intend to come across to others is the way we actually do.

Inviting feedback may help clarify whether the intentions are experienced by others in practice.

It is claimed that the vast majority of communications, the messages transmitted by us and received by others, are non-verbal. Indeed, non-verbal communication can be ten times more significant than verbal communication. The way we sit, stand, look. So much for all our talking! Our words may be appropriate and positive, but if they are conveyed from a posture of aggression or passivity then it is in this latter, non-verbal way that they are likely to be received. But even our words, if spoken with an inappropriate inflection, or muttered, or spat out, will be interpreted by the listener as imparting the meaning conveyed by the transmission.

If we frequently fail to understand why our good intentions seem to be misunderstood, it may be useful to reflect on whether this is because we are hooked into one of the roles of the bullying cycle (and thus relating from a victim or bully or rescuer or indifferent or punisher role) and/or whether the way we communicate is conveying the wrong messages.

3 Feelings: becoming emotionally literate.

(a) Telling how it feels.

In Chapter 3 I relayed how during my work with pupils I made a discovery about the feelings of everyone involved in bullying. No one involved in the bullying cycle ended up feeling good about themselves. Any short-term boost to the ego through adopting a one-up position, either by being a bully, a rescuer, a punisher, or holding oneself aloof by being indifferent, quickly faded. Attempting to boost self-esteem by putting others down is a little like taking a dose of sugar to boost energy. There is an initial surge followed by a flatness and lethargy. It is short-lived and self-defeating.

For me the most important element of the bullying cycle is enabling people to talk about how it feels for them. I believe there is enormous potential for the growth of community spirit, and that the basis for this growth is emotional honesty. There are three parts to this.

First, we have to know ourselves and recognise how we feel. This is not as easy as it might sound. What exactly are we feeling? Never mind why; just what. Can we get in touch with our feelings?

The second part is whether we can allow ourselves to admit how we feel. We may be ashamed of how we feel; or feel vulnerable about having such feelings. Hate, envy, fear, jealousy, guilt, anger. For many of us these do not come into the category of 'nice' feelings. Perhaps we don't consider them to be socially acceptable emotions, not the kind of feelings we would like to mention to others.

The third part is, of course, being able to share these feelings with someone else. There is a universal human bond of empathy, which offers a far greater potential contribution to our humanity than our ability to reason, but for many of us there is a fear that this empathy will not be there for us. Better to banish our feelings, disown them, suppress them than be banished or disowned or suppressed for sharing them. The human fear of exclusion, that most devastating of bullying strategies, inhibits our development and expression of emotions, and cuts us off from each other.

While it may seem obvious that, unless we tell someone that we feel angry or sad or hurt then they will be less able to understand us and meet our needs, our fear dominates. Fear eats the soul. It destroys our spiritual bond with each other. We have therefore a moral injunction to overcome that fear, to tell it how it is. And that means tell how it feels.

(b) Affirming self-worth.

I referred in Chapter 2 to the issue of self-loathing. Part of the antidote to that is the affirmation of self-worth. We need to give ourselves permission to feel positive and talk positively about ourselves. This is not to deny or gloss over our weaknesses, shortcomings or imperfections. None of us are or could be perfect. The purpose of this exercise is to recognise what we are good at, what we can and do offer to others, what abilities and attributes we have which we could value more highly, what potential we have yet to develop.

Rather than class this primarily as an intellectual exercise, I consider this to be fundamentally about feelings. It is not a simplistic recipe for a changed approach to the world through different thoughts. Affirmations primarily involve feelings and beliefs, and therefore are tools to tackle our main locus of resistance to change.

Affirmations are closely linked with self-esteem. We may have been brought up on negative messages: 'don't do that'; 'you're bad'; 'you're dirty'; 'you're disgusting', and so on. These negative messages are likely to have become translated into beliefs, destroying self-esteem. 'Parents are not the only ones who feed negative beliefs into children – teachers, priests, ministers and other adults and children do the same.'[32]

Affirming self-worth is the opportunity to imbue emotions into our abilities, to marvel at our gifts, to attribute a true significance to our humanity, to feel at one – neither one-up nor one-down – with ourselves and the world.

The ability for each of us to experience ourselves as a unique and wonderful human being – not just to think it or believe it, but to feel it – is enormously creative. It allows us to experience others as unique and wonderful human beings too. It also sheds us of false humility, the 'poor me' or 'I am not worthy' sentiments.

4 Actions: what we do and don't do.

We are, sadly, judged on our actions and inactions. I regard this as unfortunate and unhealthy, for two main reasons. First, what we do is not who we are, although our actions may offer clues to what we think and believe and how we feel. Secondly, judgemental attitudes presume superiority. Who are we to judge others? Consequently I have left discussion of actions and inactions to last, because I wish to ensure that what we do is not seen in a vacuum. Our actions and inactions are a physical expression of our thoughts, feelings and beliefs, particularly the latter two. The title of this book expressly points to the need for change in our actions – as parents – to overturn bullying behaviours. That of course must start with us addressing our own bullying behaviours.

The world cannot be changed by other people. It can only be changed by us. We set the example, we do not wait for others to do it for (or to) us. If we begin to change ourselves we are able to help others change too. My hope is that we can thereby inspire and encourage our children, all our hopes for the future, to be free from the destructive forces of the bullying cycle, to act differently.

There is a range of exercises that can help us to change our behaviour. These are not to be thought about: that is, they are not cerebral exercises but practical techniques. Therefore they need to be practised. Like any skill, we will get better at them the more we actually practise them, as opposed to thinking about practising them.

(a) Relaxation and stress release.

The state of tension in our bodies is of considerable importance. There are several reasons for this. First, it may reflect pent-up emotions which would be better expressed. Repressed emotion is considered physically damaging as it can increase tension and stress within the body (among other symptoms). Excessive levels of stress contribute to unease and disease of vital organs, including the heart.

Secondly, our capacity to cope with further emotions while suffering from excessive tension and stress is inhibited. We will be more likely to act and react in negative and unhealthy ways. That is, we are more prone to adopting one of the roles in the bullying cycle (such as victim – 'I can't cope'; bully – 'I'll sort you out good and proper'; punisher – 'you'll pay for giving me hassle'; indifferent – 'I really can't be bothered with you'; and rescuer – 'that's it, you just stay in your room and then it won't happen again').

Thirdly, while our bodies need to have a balance of tension

and relaxation, like breathing in and breathing out, too much tension disables the body from functioning. Therefore, being able to control our bodies, preventing them from reverting to a physical state which disables constructive negotiation of stressful encounters, becomes an important component of our strategy. There is a number of ways in which this can be assisted. You may find some of the following helpful:

• *Tension and relaxation exercise.* One of the exercises I do with young people in schools is to ask them to gradually tense up all their muscles, from their feet to the heads; and then try and walk across the floor. It is actually a physical impossibility.

Alongside the tensing of muscles comes the imbalance of breathing; either not breathing at all, or quick, shallow, panting breaths. Palms become sweaty; the heart starts beating fast. It is a re-creation of the impact that fear has on the body. The buildup of this tension – physically this adrenalin – reaches a point where it needs to explode. This is the moment of fight or flight. While this may be a legacy of earlier times when survival was dependent on the need to respond at a fight or flight level, by and large it is a physical relic of little contemporary benefit.

The exercise continues by encouraging pupils to repeatedly tense and relax all their muscles, working their way up the body from feet to head, and breathing deeply and regularly. They are helped to be in touch with their bodily functioning. 'What is happening to your body now?' To consolidate this exercise I later incorporate it into the assertiveness exercises (see below) and check whether the pupils can retain their calm, relaxed body posture and breathing when role-playing a confrontation.

• *Guided fantasy.* A period of calm where, with one person (or if alone a tape recording) taking on the task of talking through a particular relaxing fantasy (my two favourite sequences are travelling through the air on a magic carpet, from take off then floating away through to landing; and lying on a beach, entering the sea and re-emerging to lie quietly on the sand), the others lie still, flat on their backs, close their eyes and experience the journey. This can have a very powerful calming effect.

Because being calm is something we do not always feel either sufficiently valuable ('it's wasting time') or comfortable with ('what if someone sees me?'), I find that people are generally more tense than they need be. Recognising and getting in touch with the rhythms of the seasons, the day and the body has an effective harmonising effect. I use a guided fantasy at the start of all my rhythmic groupwork sessions with disturbed adolescents (based on a breathing-out, breathing-in, breathing-out cycle of: calm – engage – explore – create – reflect – relax).

- *Oh-oh.* In the film *The Rain Man*, Dustin Hoffman played a hospital patient with autism. At moments when he became anxious (for whatever reason, such as being late) he would recognise his distress and say, 'Oh-oh.'

However, in this case the 'oh-oh' alerted others to his distress. What I am suggesting is that the 'oh-oh' is said inside our heads to recognise that, perhaps for reasons we do not immediately understand, our bodies are becoming tense. Our breathing has stopped or become fast and shallow, our heart is beating faster, and so on.

Whatever has triggered our tension needs to be met and countered with injunctions and affirmations for us to remain calm or regain composure, and therefore enable ourselves to handle the situation as positively as we can. The most important thing at this stage is not to analyse the specific source of the tension (that is a thinking task to be done later) but to prevent it from becoming disabling.

- *Injunctions.* A set of commands which you can use to tell yourself to relax and stay in control, such as 'count to ten'; 'keep calm'; 'stay cool'; 'don't rise to the bait'; 'don't let him/her/them get to me'; 'I don't need to react to this'; and so on. You will probably find expressions of your own that work for you. But they need to be your injunctions, not the commands of someone else. Their purpose is to help you remain calm.

• *Affirmations.* These are 'used to counter and flush out negative beliefs'.[33] Affirmations are reassuring phrases which you can say within your head or post up around the house to help you feel better about yourself when fearful or under threat. They are reminders of your good points and your ability to cope, and should be particularly addressed to those messages, those aspects of self-belief that undermine your confidence. Examples include: 'I'm OK'; 'I'm still a good person'; 'I can handle this'; 'I will be fine'; 'come on, I'll take this steady and I'll be OK'; 'this isn't about me, just remember that'; and so on. Again, you will no doubt find expressions of your own that will help you. Even how you say them to yourself is important. If they sound unconvincing and tentative to you, it suggests you don't really believe them. Practice – which means repetition – is vital. The impact when they are working for you will be experienced in your feelings and beliefs and demonstrated through your actions. You will be stronger and more able to resist being hooked into the bullying cycle.

• *Saying 'No'.* This is one of the simplest yet most effective ways of responding to the buildup of tension in a stressful encounter, as well as being an assertiveness tactic of more general use. Retain regular breathing and quietly but clearly intone the word 'no' while breathing out, keeping the body calm, facing straight onto the other person, and with eyes firmly fixed on (without staring at) the other person. In a situation where there is a deliberate intention of winding you up (hooking you into the bullying cycle), there is a need to refrain from excessive dialogue and instead convey the message that you do not want to play the game. Saying 'no' calmly and repeatedly may achieve the result of remaining in control of your body and your fear, and getting the message across.

(b) Assertiveness Exercises.

Following on from the above exercises there are four specific assertiveness techniques that I consistently find helpful. Assertiveness 'is not a character trait with which some people come into this world and others do not. It is a communication skill and, like any other skill, can be learned'.[34]

In contradiction of some writers who only consider assertiveness training useful for victims, I am clear that assertiveness training is helpful for all of us. The reason for this is that we are open to all the roles of the bullying cycle, not just one, and the purpose of being assertive is to relate on an equal level, to be neither one-up or one-down. Therefore learning to be assertive helps us when we would otherwise be aggressive and one-up, such as when we bully, rescue, are indifferent or punish. Assertiveness helps us not to be passive and one-down, such as when we are victim or bystander.

There are four techniques outlined below and each may prove more productive in different kinds of situations rather than generally, so I have given some examples of when I suggest they can be used.

• *Broken record.* This technique is useful when someone is attempting to provoke a response which hooks you into the bullying cycle. Situations can include when a person is being aggressive, such as refusing to return an item of yours; or being obstructive. They may be seeking out a victim or punisher. Or perhaps someone is being a victim, pleading and beseeching, trying to elicit a rescuing or bullying response from you.

The technique of broken record is to demand what you want or state your position in an assertive manner, conscious of body posture, the words you use, the tone of voice, and the facial expression; and keep repeating the demand or statement in an identical way until it has been heard and understood. Perseverance is required (in particular avoid sighing) as it is essential in this technique that there is absolutely no change in the words, tone or body language.

Because this technique is persistently assertive, the other person (who is inviting either a one-down response from you – a passive, victim role, or a competitive one-up role – an aggressive or punitive or rescuing role) will realise the futility of continuing. However, be aware that a change of communication from the other person may be an alternative attempt to hook you – for example, a change from being aggressive (a bully) to being passive and pitiful (a victim).

• *Fogging.* This technique may be particularly helpful when you are subjected to verbal abuse, such as name-calling and 'slagging'. The idea is to defuse the impact intended by the abuser by assertively taking on the insult and making a joke of it – but not making a joke out of yourself. A former colleague of mine, Iain Stoddart, was an arch-exponent of this. He had the ability to be confronted with the most aggressive and threatening verbal abuse and take all the sting out of it. By not responding at the one-down level (the victim) or the one-up level (counter-aggression) he retained his power in the situation and dissipated the abuse in fog. Some of the examples of this I've used, illustrated in *To Bully No More! The Pupil Pack*, are:

'Baldy, baldy.'

'Bald? Sure. But then why hide brains. If you've got them flaunt them.'

'There goes four eyes.'

'What do you mean four eyes? Look, here's my clip-on shades. Six eyes, isn't it? Now that's what I call cool.'

'You smell.'

'I know, that's what I use my nose for, surely you must smell too.'

• *Sensitive assertion.* This is a most powerful and important technique as it recognises and appreciates the feelings of the other person as well as your own. This is particularly useful when faced with someone's aggression, for example when expressed in anger or displeasure about something you have (or have not) done. How many times do we see an attack responded to by a counter-attack and the problem and tension and hurt feelings escalate?

The first part of this sensitive assertion technique acknowledges that you can appreciate how the other person feels. That in itself often dissipates much of the anger and aggression. But then you still assert your own position, neither resorting to

empty promises (never intending to fulfil them) which I interpret as another form of aggression, nor acquiescing to the
other's demands, nor making excuses as a victim might do – 'it
wasn't me' or 'it wasn't my fault'.

An example of this technique might be:

'Every time you arrange to see me you turn up late. I'm
really sick of it. Who do you think you are?'

'I can understand why you feel so fed up with me. I'd feel
like that in your position too. However, I was expecting a
'phone call and I chose to wait for it, even though I knew I
would be late for our meeting.'

'Well how do you think I feel? You'd better not do it again.'

'I can tell you feel angry and hurt. I want you to understand
that meeting with you is important to me. However, I won't
promise never to be late again, but I can assure you it would
only be for what I consider to be a good reason. I hope you
can accept that.'

Sensitive assertion is the Adult talking (in terms of
Transactional Analysis' Parent-Adult-Child). While this does
not imply that it is a form of discourse to be used exclusively
by adults (as there is a Parent, Adult and Child in all of us), I
have found parents and teachers confused and uncomfortable
with this kind of approach being used by young people, especially because it is so powerful. It seems too mature (even
allowing for the language not being as full and articulate as
the example given). It can induce wariness and anxiety and
suspicion in some adults: 'is this a wind-up?'; 'what's all this
about?'; 'I don't understand what's happening'.

Unfortunately this is actually an indication of the overwhelming prevalence of the bullying cycle. It is not a straight-
forward process of one person becoming assertive and
everyone else allowing and responding positively to it.
Indeed, acts of assertion can actually adversely affect relationships at first, as those on the receiving end may well
become more aggressive. This is an expression of fear and confusion and resistance to change. As assertiveness is not on the
same continuum as passivity and aggression, there is a fear of

what this new form of communication means, and an attempt is made to hook the victim back into an understood and recognisable role.

Being confronted by a young person not wanting to be hooked into the adult's game can therefore be unnerving. Consequently there is a tendency for the adult wrongly to categorise assertive responses as cheek (that is, aggression), and to respond accordingly. This ties in with a belief system enshrining the need to be one-up. 'Don't let them get the upper hand'; 'give them an inch and they'll take a mile'; 'let them see who's boss'; 'don't let them get away with it'; and so on. In the educational world it also links with the edicts to 'be on your guard', 'stay in control', 'be firm' and that favourite instruction regarding non-verbal communication with a new class – 'never smile before Christmas'.

For adults who can only perceive the world in terms of those who are aggressive and those who are passive, coming face to face with this kind of assertiveness is confusing and often frightening. Although human beings are very adept at change, we are also anxious about and resistant to it. New experiences are translated initially into old patterns of understanding.

- *Escalating assertion.* This technique 'ups the odds' to achieve the outcome, but without ever becoming aggressive. In effect it is a way of continuing to assert individual rights in the face of oppression. One particular situation where this can be used effectively is when taking goods back to a shop. For example:

'Excuse me, I bought this toaster from you and it doesn't work.'

'It was fine when I sold it.'

'The toaster was in its box when you sold it to me. As soon as I took it out and tried it, it didn't work. Please replace it or give me a refund.'

'Clear off, I'm sick of people like you coming in here complaining.'

'Please don't speak to me like that. Either replace the

toaster or give me a refund now, or else fetch the manager for me.'

'The manager's not here, and I've got other things to do. Shove off.'

'In that case I will contact Trading Standards and seek their assistance.'

'Oh, all right, here you are. Here's another toaster.'

At no time was there a threat such as 'if you don't do what I want, your windows will get smashed'. Throughout the tone and words were assertive. While it is very hard to contend with aggression being directed at you, it does not help – despite claims from those who have succeeded in bullying their way to an outcome – to resort to counter-aggression. It may be that, in the example above, counter-aggression could sometimes obtain a replacement toaster. But this would be achieved only at the expense of being hooked into the bullying cycle.

Assertiveness, as well as not necessarily having an immediately positive impact, is often 'over-done' at first and comes out as aggression. For those of us brought up on the passive–aggressive continuum, it is as hard for us to break the mould as it is for those with whom we relate. Again I emphasise that we are always in relationships, and the expectations of others as to how we behave within these relationships is a critical factor in inducing and producing our roles and transactions. Changing the way we relate and the way others relate to us requires practice. In the way we have trained each other to behave in passive and aggressive ways, we need to retrain ourselves and others to become assertive.

> People can become threatened by change in others for many different reasons. It is not so important to ask why others oppose changes in your behaviour, but more important to ask yourself, 'How am I going to cope with it?' It is a trap to focus on the other person. What we need to do is to look at ourselves. The way in which we change, develop and grow is by looking at our own behaviour and emotions, not other people's.[35]

However, the importance of assertiveness is not only that it feels good and helps the individual develop confidence and self-esteem, and the capacity to be more responsible. It also enhances the self-esteem of those on the receiving end of the assertive behaviour. It is effectively a 'no lose' form of behaviour.

As I explained at the start of this chapter, there is a need for parents to know themselves – their beliefs, thoughts, feelings and actions. There is a need for parents to be able to address their desire to change, to give it physical expression and thereby to provide a role model for their children. Engaging assertively with our children is an effective basis for self-enhancing and child-enhancing relationships to be fostered.

The questions and exercises included above in this chapter are designed to help parents work at this at an individual level. But these exercises are relevant for young people too, dependent on their age and level of understanding. I have undertaken all these above exercises with children, including those with learning disabilities, from the age of seven years upwards.

> I believe that the most difficult person for us to face is *ourselves* and in changing, that is who we are up against. It is important to realise and understand that in changing, a great deal of resistance comes from within ourselves.[36]

If we have taken on the challenge to change ourselves and have begun working on these exercises as part of our daily life, we will need help to overcome this resistance – our resistance. There is now another step. This step requires us to seek support.

Exercises

Getting started.

What problems do you anticipate in tackling the individual exercises identified in this chapter?

What difficulties do you anticipate in introducing the

reasons for you undertaking these exercises to other members of your family? How might they respond to you?

How would you feel – and how would you respond to other family members – if they began to use these kinds of exercises to change themselves?

Is it possible for you to undertake these exercises alongside other people?

Case Examples

Issue 5: Breaking the cycle in practice

The case examples are not untypical illustrations of young people in relationships in schools.

How would you set about helping them to break the bullying cycle in each of those cases?

How would you use your knowledge of the importance of beliefs and feelings, thoughts and actions, as well as roles, to inform your intervention?

CHAPTER 6

I CAN'T DO IT ON MY OWN!

It is absolutely true, of course, that no one person can change the world on his or her own. Or, to be more accurate, no one can change everybody else's world. But any change we make in ourselves – in our beliefs, thoughts, feelings, actions – does affect other people. Family members are likely to be affected most. How they respond (and how you respond to their changes) is of vital importance.

The bullying cycle is habit-forming. It is also addictive. Therefore we can usefully consider breaking the bullying cycle habit in the context of how we might break other bad habits. In my case, I will illustrate the difficulties I had in giving up smoking and the lessons this provided for me about breaking out of the bullying cycle.

I began to smoke to feel accepted by (and acceptable to) other young people. At first I didn't like it. It made me unwell. But I choked back the distaste and stuck with it. Soon it didn't seem so bad. I flaunted my cigarettes and my new-found ability to smoke. I denied to myself that smoking would do me any harm. After all, I was young, with many years ahead of me. My Dad had smoked for years and seemed fit and healthy. I would be OK. I mixed well socially, and as a student at college I became established among a group of friends whose company I found entertaining and instructive. We regularly and frequently went to the student bar and drank beer – and smoked cigarettes.

Somehow I never quite accepted the belief that smoking was unproblematic. I spent a lot of money on it, which I could ill afford. I also became unfit, a contrast to my childhood when I engaged enthusiastically in a number of sports. There was also a cultural change in process. Cigarette advertising was banned on TV. One or two people in my acquaintance (but not in my social circle) began to speak out against it.

At some point – I cannot remember it being a single moment – I must have taken stock of my situation. I did not believe smoking was good for me. I did not accept it was good for my father either as he constantly coughed (he later died of lung cancer). I had limited money and did not want to spend so much on cigarettes. I did not feel good about my physical health and lack of fitness. I understood the risks of continuing to smoke. I knew I could stop smoking by saying 'no'. I decided that I would stop. My beliefs, thoughts, feelings and actions were united. To be fair I had some trepidation about change, but essentially I saw it as a positive challenge. I would be a non-smoker and proud of it.

I announced to my friends that I had decided to stop smoking. They seemed a little encouraging, certainly not hostile, but mostly indifferent. In fact we went to the pub, me intending to celebrate. They all smoked of course, as we always did when we went to the pub. During the social conversation, cigarettes were liberally shared around. I was offered one several times by friends who had already forgotten (or ignored the fact) that I had given up. Before long I was persuaded just to have one. After all, a gradual giving-up process might be more effective than a sudden shock to the system. I smoked two, three, four, and by the end of the evening felt compelled to buy another packet to repay people who had given me cigarettes. But once this packet was finished, that would be it. No more.

Over the next four months I gave up cigarettes seventeen times. The final and successful seventeenth attempt was when I moved away from the college, from the area and from my friends. I started a course at a university some fifty miles away from my social circle. Somehow, despite sixteen failed attempts, I still retained the belief that it was possible to give up smoking. I also retained the desire to do so, even though by now my confidence in my ability to give it up was very low. But as it happened it was easy. By breaking with all my friends and our familiar patterns of behaviour, I broke with smoking.

Was moving away the price I had to pay? At no time when I was with my friends was I able to say that they pressurised me into continuing to smoke. Sure they offered me cigarettes, but there were no jibes or taunts. Looking back, I now realise they did in fact undermine me. They did that because they did not change their behaviour at all. They were unsupportive of my attempts to give up smoking by being indifferent. They did not take me seriously. They did not extend their friendship to cope with my desire and need to change. They did not help me gain the confidence to follow through my resolution.

I later wondered whether they were real friends. Perhaps their company was fun, but socialising with them was at the expense of my individuality. But that was unfair. The lesson for me was that there is a limit to how much we can change ourselves, even if we remove ambivalent and ambiguous beliefs, thoughts, feelings and actions. For even without such potentially mixed messages we need other people's support to help us. We are not in a social vacuum. We are not designed to be self-reliant. We need to acknowledge our inter-dependence, our need for help.

I have a fundamental problem with the popular notion that we are – and should be – independent. In this view, dependency is to be shunned at all costs, and is seen as a sign of failure. I agree that it is neither desirable nor healthy to be in a state of total dependency. This is a victim position, and one that strips away much of a person's dignity. But the other extreme is independence, which is a form of social isolation and detachment. It is an anomie. It is also, generally, a denial of the real situation. It is a pretence, a claim that we do not need other people.

What I wish to put forward, as both a realistic analysis of

existing human society and as an expression of an ideal form of association, is the notion of mutual inter-dependence. We need other people to help us live our lives to the full, in physical, emotional, recreational, commercial, educational and spiritual senses. Other people need us. We all have a significant contribution to give and to receive. The quality of our society is a factor of our abilities – our collective and individual abilities – to be open to receive and open to give.

The spirit of giving requires a spirit of receiving. Indeed, there is a spirit within the gift. An acknowledgement of that gift as a bond of our common humanity, of our spiritual unity, is the acknowledgement of our mutual inter-dependence.

Before we can attain a position where we can truly experience our mutual inter-dependence, we first have to acknowledge the cultural context in which we both want to change ourselves and seek the supports necessary for us to do so. We need to come to terms with the reality that we may find it hard, as I did when trying to give up smoking, to ask for and obtain the support of family members and friends as their beliefs and behaviour may be in contradiction to our desired change. This is particularly the case when we attempt to go against the grain, against the received wisdom and the socially acceptable way. Even more so if we set ourselves against the existing social order.

The basis of this lack of support may be seen as disrespect. This disrespect may itself be based on fear and self-loathing. Alice Miller bluntly details the problem we have to confront in ourselves and in our society, as well as pointing up again the pervasive nature of the bullying cycle within the social order.

> Disrespect is the weapon of the weak and a defence against one's own despised and unwanted feelings, which could trigger memories of events in one's repressed history. And the fountainhead of all contempt, all discrimination, is the more or less conscious, controlled, and covert exercise of power over the child by the adult. Except in the case of murder or serious bodily harm, this unrestrained use of power is tolerated by society; what adults do to their child's spirit is entirely their own affair, for the child is

regarded as the parents' property in the same way as the citizens of a totalitarian state are considered the property of its government.

Until we become sensitised to the small child's suffering, this wielding of power by adults will continue to be regarded as a normal aspect of the human condition, for hardly anyone pays attention to it or takes it seriously. Because the victims are 'only children', their distress is trivialised. But in twenty years time these children will be adults who will feel compelled to pay it all back to their own children. They may consciously fight with vigour against cruelty in the world yet carry within themselves an experience of cruelty that they may unconsciously inflict on others. . . .

It is absolutely urgent that people become aware of the degree to which this disrespect of children is persistently transmitted from one generation to the next, perpetuating destructive behaviour.[37]

I referred in my Introduction to the scale of child sexual abuse, the vast majority of which is perpetrated by family members and never subjected to criminal investigation and prosecution. Even though we may know more about the extent of child sexual abuse now, this doesn't mean we are any more able or willing to stop it happening. If the destructive use of power by parents over their children is an inherent part of our value system, how will we find people to support us to relinquish our abuse of power over our children? Are other parents committed to change too?

Within any social order, within any organisation or system, the bullying cycle can thrive. Abuse within the family is rife, and the roles will be seen. An aggressive, physically and sexually abusive mother may be complemented by a father who is a bystander or indifferent, while the child continues to be a victim. Or an abusive father is complemented by a mother who rescues her child. Or a child who seeks redress and punishment for the abuse committed by one parent may be punished by the other parent who rescues the partner who abused the child in the first place. And so on.

Peck states that families can be sterile, oppressive institutions, for 'families, like all other systems, are systems. Systems resist change. Break with a family tradition and no wonder the system will fight back. You have to upset the balance of things, and the family norms may have to change.'[38] Physical, sexual and emotional abuse is too often a 'family tradition'. It is a tradition that is highly resistant to change.

It seems to me that the basis of all resistance to change is fear. Resistance to change can produce behaviours which ridicule and undermine those who either promote change or inspire change through their own example. This is one way of overcoming fear, by removing the sources of it through suppression, oppression or extinction. However, historically all attempts at oppression and suppression of others, whatever the degrees of brutality and however widespread, have eventually collapsed. It is a destructive but eventually futile way of attempting to overcome fear, self-doubt and self-loathing.

Bullying of children can be seen as the most pernicious, most widespread and ultimately most destructive form of oppression ever experienced for everyone involved in the bullying cycle, as it condemns so much of our futures. But like other world-wide instances of oppression, bullying can and will collapse if the forces for change are strong.

The alternative to resistance through fear is to overcome fear by going with it. If what is fearful is addressed, engaged, and seen as a challenge and opportunity for growth, the fear fades and is removed. Then the scope for change is immense. The positive way to overcome fear and hence to effect change is through love.

'There is no room for fear in love.' (*Scottish Episcopal Liturgy*, 1982)

The ability to love is the basis of our inter-connectedness, our humanity. It is fear which prevents us from loving. It is fear that feeds our feelings of loneliness, guilt, anxiety, anger, frustration, sadness and vulnerability. Fear also engenders excitement, the physical rush of adrenalin. The bullying cycle thrives on fear.

My friends who did not support me in stopping smoking did

not love me. They liked me, they found me good company, but they did not extend themselves to support my growth as a person – especially if that growth posed threats for themselves, and undermined their confidence further by calling into question, albeit implicitly, their behaviour. My attempt to give up smoking fed their vulnerabilities, their guilt, their anxieties, their lack of self-esteem and their fears. Their fear prevented them from loving me.

But every time we fail to respond to the chance to love someone else, we feel worse about ourselves and fall further into the trap of the bullying cycle. We fail again to love ourselves. To be precise, we do indeed love our neighbour as ourselves, in that we are as full of self-loathing as loathing of others. Of course, we generally have the social graces and etiquette to disguise these feelings, so that they seep out or emerge in clever, subtle ways rather than in an explosion of rage and hatred. This doesn't mean that we are any less destructive, far from it. We are not even open and honest.

To whom can a person turn when finding themselves the victim of a dishonest, superficially sophisticated bully: one who destroys with his eyebrows rather than his fists? If we live in a social climate which demands justice and evidence of actions, and where fear prevails, who would dare tell that they were being bullied in such a way? But if we lived in a climate which was based on love, we would have no need to be afraid.

By love I don't mean affection, and certainly not lust. Love is a commitment to extend ourselves to assist the spiritual growth of others. To love one's neighbour is to commit oneself to supporting their well-being and personal development. It doesn't mean we have to like them. The edict to love is based fundamentally on our Christian faith.

> Leave no claim outstanding against you, except that of mutual love. He who loves his neighbour has satisfied every claim of the law. For the commandments, 'Thou shalt not commit adultery, thou shalt not kill, thou shall not steal, thou shalt not covet', and any other commandments there may be, are all summed up in the one rule, 'Love your neighbour as yourself.' Love cannot wrong a

neighbour; therefore the whole law is summed up in love. (Rom 13: 8-10, NEB.)

Canon Crosfield, in his Lenten sermon delivered at St James The Less Church in Penicuik in 1996, introduced us to a set of five precepts which encapsulate the potential healing of relationships through empathic love. These are: recognise, respect, listen, understand and reconcile. They comprise stages in the healing process of empathic reconciliation. Empathy is the practical expression of love. From the foundation of beliefs, thoughts, feelings and actions, empathy translates our love into practice.

I will elaborate on the five precepts in turn.

- *Recognise.* By that we appreciate our inter-connectedness as human beings. We are, we exist in common. Recognising people as unique but fellow human beings created by God allows us to resist the urge to defend ourselves against others, labelling and dismissing them as 'the enemy', 'bad', 'evil', 'wrong', 'bullies'. Our ability to recognise requires us to see them as equal in the eyes of God, sharing the same commonality in God.

- *Respect.* Other people have a right to disagree with us. They have valid viewpoints, and whether or not we find them compatible or congruent with ours should not detract from the respect we accord any other person. We may not like or welcome their opinions, but we can still respect the person who has them. This requires us to have an intellectual and emotional awareness that an unwelcome or uncomfortable action by someone does not mean they require less respect as people.

- *Listen.* This is the consequence of respecting others. Listening is not the dismissive 'I hear what you say', but a genuine attempt to take in what is being conveyed – verbally and in particular non-verbally. This physical task of listening is active not passive and it can be exhausting. It also requires an emotional and physical commitment, and a belief that really hearing and seeing other people is important.

- *Understand.* Although this is primarily an intellectual awareness of others, based on recognising and respecting them, listening to and seeing them, a deeper understanding can now be gleaned. Our ability to empathise assumes an ability to travel alongside, which a true understanding can enable.

- *Reconcile.* The spiritual hope for the world lies in our endeavours to reconcile, to express our love for each other so that we do not use our energies to divide, oppress, overpower, condemn and humiliate, which shrivels us all as human beings, reducing us (as Canon Crosfield vividly portrayed in another sermon) to BOMs and WOWs: Bitter Old Men and Wicked Old Women.

Reconciliation is so hard, so painful. We fear reconciliation for it is inextricably linked with forgiveness. 'Forgive those who trespass against us.' As if it was that easy. It requires a tremendous act of love of our fellow human beings. Yet do we not yearn to be forgiven ourselves, to allow us to shed our burden of self-loathing? Reconciliation allows us all to grow, and further develops our abilities to recognise, respect, listen, understand and reconcile. It is a spiritual spiral.

Younger children are often more open to reconciliation than adults. But then they learn from us. So often parents and children are disabled through fear from dealing with bullying. Fear of reprisals, of punishment, of vilification, of making things worse, of upsetting the social order, of being seen as being weak, of being deemed neurotic and over-protective, of being divisive – and fundamentally fear of blame. Blame is the antithesis of love.

The work of Barbara Maines and George Robinson has been very influential in addressing the problem of blame in dealing with bullying.[39] A 'blame culture' is irresponsible. It precludes the growth and development of individual and collective responsibility. The attraction of blame is that it allows us to abdicate responsibility.

In allocating blame to someone else we play the roles of victim (inasmuch as we claim no power over the situation) and bully (inasmuch as we stigmatise and vilify the object of blame) and punisher (inasmuch as we use or abuse our power to impose or invoke sanctions). We also expend much effort in deflecting blame away from ourselves onto others, unless we choose to absorb and carry it (*mea culpa*).

Chains or sequences of beliefs, thoughts, feelings and actions from the standpoint of seeing and ascribing blame can be identified.[40] The blame sequences are of three kinds:

(1) Event – blame other person – anger – frustration – indignant and self-righteous – aggression.
(2) Event – blame other person – anger – frustration – feelings not expressed – passive aggression.
(3) Event – blame self – self-conscious and embarrassed – low self-esteem – passivity.

The 'blame game' is an integral part of the bullying cycle. All the roles thrive on the existence of blame. Indeed, a 'no blame' approach undermines the foundations of the bullying cycle by removing the fear of blame and allowing responsibility to be taken and accepted.

The antidote to the blame/no responsibility matrix exercise I undertake with children in schools is the no blame/responsibility matrix. In this exercise the 'blame questions' (why? who? when? what? how?) are avoided and replaced by a set of questions designed to seek clarification and enlightenment and offer help.[41]

Examples of these questions are:

- 'I would like to help. Is there anything I can do?'
- 'Is there anything we all need to understand which would help us sort out this situation?'
- 'Is there anything you can do or would like to do?'
- 'Is there anyone else who can help or who might like to help?'
- 'Can you think of anything that might help prevent these kinds of situations happening again?'

An ethos of mutual and shared responsibility in resolving the situation replaces the ethos of allocating and apportioning blame. The responses to these questions tend to be constructive: 'Yes'; 'I have an idea'; 'I could help by. . .'; 'I think my parent/friend/teacher could help as well. I will ask them'; and so on.

The reaction of most young people to this exercise is extremely positive. They welcome the chance to become involved in resolving a difficult and unhappy situation once they are freed from their fear of being blamed. Some are less sure at first, in the same way that people can distrust assertive responses (as I stated earlier) from those whose normal and expected communications have generally been passive or aggressive.

There are three very apparent reasons why young people's responses are positive to this type of assertive and engaging questioning. The first reason is that the questioner comes across as genuinely concerned to resolve the situation – a situation which it is accepted may involve many people in different ways – rather than allocate blame. Each communication is honest. Each person is approaching the situation from an equal position. That is, the framework for these communications is not founded on 'one-up' or 'one-down' interactions.

The second reason for the positive response to this approach to dealing with the bullying cycle is that it is based on responsibility. Responsibility is ownership, not in the sense of being blameworthy but in having control over beliefs, thoughts, feelings and actions. In truth if I am responsible I own myself, I am not owned by anyone else. Responsibility, rather than being a burden, can be experienced as freedom.

The third reason for the children's positive response is that it is not grounded on justice and punishment or vengeance and retribution. While adults tend to extol the merits of sanctions and imposed discipline, of being seen to be fair and just, children are more astute and more in touch with their needs.

When bullying is taking place, whoever else is involved, wherever it happens, however terrifying and awful it may be for them and whichever role they may be in at the time, there is consistently only one thing that young people want and need: *they want the bullying to stop*.

Stopping the bullying cycle is the only desired and necessary solution. It is no solution at all to continue the cycle with other people in the various roles, which is what happens in the 'justice model'. The role of sanctions or punishment or vengeance or blood money is to perpetuate a set of unhealthy relationships, to retain the status quo.

Indeed, anthropologists of the 'functionalist school' refer to the 'checks and balances' between tribes or societies, actions and reactions that keep the same kinds of relationships established between them. However, just because a pattern of relationships remains stable does not mean it is a healthy pattern. We cannot presume the relationships are based on love rather than fear.

So what makes us so afraid of love? Are we really able to love ourselves? Are we really able to love our children?

The problem may be that we do not experience ourselves as being loved or, indeed, even of being lovable. If we are full of self-loathing how can we extend ourselves and offer the love that others require? If this is the case, so much of what I have said about love throughout this chapter will be meaningless, liable to be dismissed as glib and precious musings, not 'real'.

I can understand that reaction. I have been in that place. It is a place I can easily return to. I have no special indemnity or immunity from fear, from self-loathing, from the bullying cycle. What I have, indeed what I need to have, is a faith that, whatever and whoever I am, I am loved. When I fail to experience that love from other people, whether because I am no longer open to that gift or because it is not being offered, and when I feel I have no love to offer others, I need to turn to my other, ultimate parent: 'God is love and we are his children. . . . We love because he loved us first.' (*Scottish Episcopal Liturgy*, 1982.)

How hard it is to hold onto the belief in God's love when we are in pain. Bullying is painful, whichever role we play in the bullying cycle. The cover of this book pictures a child with a tear. I cannot be sure why the child is sad. What I see is a child in pain. When I see that pain I cannot differentiate my response dependent on whether it is that child who has bullied or who is a victim, or who fears for a friend, or who has witnessed bullying. What I can see is a child who has a reason to doubt love, whether parental love, the love of friends, or God's love. Our experience of pain challenges our faith and our relationship with God.[42]

If we cannot hold onto the certainty of God's love, then we are disabled – we disable ourselves – from loving ourselves and from loving others. Pain (and the fear of pain) attacks our beliefs about the world, and calls us to question what kind of God would allow us and our children to experience such torments. A caring God would surely not allow his children to suffer.

Christians have struggled to understand the role of pain, especially in the face of accusations that pain is the apparent contradiction of God's love and purpose for us. But there is something about pain that is important for us to understand as Christians, and which will also help us to appreciate the lessons we have learnt about the bullying cycle too.

First, pain is not about divine retribution. I do not believe pain is God's punishment for our individual wrong-doings. God is not a punisher.

Secondly, particular pains are not specially selected out for us by God. We are not victims of God's will to see us suffer. God is not a bully.

Thirdly, pain is not removed from us because we believe in God. We have no special dispensation, and our prayers will not allow us to escape from pain. God is not a rescuer.

Fourthly, because we suffer pain we should not presume God has left us. We endure the pain. But when our children suffer we hurt too. Badly, deeply. We are involved in our children's suffering. So too is God involved in our suffering. God is not indifferent.

Fifthly, when we are most sorely afflicted we struggle to

have faith in God. God appears impotent. It is then that we need our faith, our trust that God is not a bystander.

God is our supporter, to help us bear the pain, to support our healing, to help us to learn from our pain, and to work to prevent unnecessary pain for ourselves and others. God is our faith that a society based on love is possible.

The pain of bullying is immense. The history of the last days of Jesus' life presents us with a lesson on bullying. Jesus was teased and tormented, and derided by priests. He did not put himself forward as a victim, and often confounded his bullies. For example, Jesus did not fall for the priests' trick of getting him to advocate the non-payment of taxes. Instead he said, 'Give unto Caesar what is Caesar's and give unto God what is God's.'

Jesus was betrayed by a friend, an action which led to the culmination of the bullying of Jesus, and a betrayal that so affected Judas that, full of guilt for his bullying action, he committed suicide. Subsequently a judge tried to rescue Jesus, but Jesus continued to assert himself. Pontius Pilate then became indifferent, he washed his hands of him. One of Jesus' closest friends, Simon Peter, stood by and denied he knew Jesus.

Jesus was crucified, humiliated further by being adorned with a crown of thorns. Jesus' death was protracted. As any parent would suffer, so too did God as his child Jesus died slowly on the cross. But Jesus still knew the suffering of his tormentors to be no less significant than his own, and he prayed for their forgiveness. At one point Jesus, in the height of his pain, doubted the presence of God's love: 'hast thou forsaken me?'

God expressed, through the sufferings of Jesus, that we could not be immune and protected from pain, and he graphically portrayed the pain of bullying. The love of God was to be with his child, not to take the pain away, but to suffer with him. This was the way God showed his love: 'God so loved the world.'

We are free to choose how we live. We are free to believe, to think, to act, to feel. God has given us an understanding of bullying, and an opportunity to learn from the pain of Jesus. Our faith does not need to be blind, but informed by the light of Jesus' experience and God's way of loving. God did not take the pain away, he did not make Jesus immune to pain. Jesus' passion allowed us to witness the real essence of compassion: to suffer with someone, alongside someone. Compassion and empathy are fundamental qualities of our humanity and of our Christianity. We can only draw on these qualities if we have the self-belief, the self-worth and the self-confidence that emanates from an appreciation and understanding of God's love for us.

God also shows us the strength we can receive from our faith. The way God's love is expressed does not belittle us, but raises our status. God has made us free to choose because we are worthwhile, because we are important. He outlines the consequences of our choices and our consciences, but does not dictate our actions.

God is beside us because we are important. Likewise our children are important to us. We cannot live their lives for them, however much we may want to protect them from mistakes and suffering. Instead we can love them in an empowering way, because they matter for themselves. We can walk beside them, neither in front nor behind. We can express our compassion and empathy. As God loves us, so can we love them.

Exercises

Supporting the supporters.

I would like you to consider how you give and receive support. How is the gift of love, care and support experienced? Is there a sense of spirituality within the gift?

You may wish to reflect on particular instances of when you have been supported by others. Were they rescuing you; or were they giving you their unconditional love?

How did you feel in receiving their support?

Perhaps you may wish to reflect now on how you give support and love to others. How do you feel when you offer this gift? Are you angry or upset if it is not wanted, or not wanted in a particular way or at a particular time? Or relieved because it was essentially only a gesture? Or do you feel that your love is still as secure, still as available?

We need to give and receive support. I invite you to identify whom you support and how you are supported to support them. Who is involved in this process and how does it happen? How explicit are you in seeking support, and are you able to receive it?

If you cannot receive love, caring and support, there is little chance that you will be able to give it. Should you consistently resist offers of support you will be denying other people your love.

Case Examples

Issue 6: Loving young people.

How would you introduce the notion of love to the young people in each of the examples?

What are your fears about doing this?

What supports would you need to be able to do this?

CHAPTER 7

SO WHAT DO WE DO WITH THE CHILDREN?

Life is difficult.

This is a great truth, one of the greatest truths. . . . Most do not fully see this truth that life is difficult. Instead they moan more or less incessantly, noisily or subtly, about the enormity of their problems, their burdens, and their difficulties as if life were generally easy, as if life *should* be easy. . . .

Life is a series of problems. Do we want to moan about them or solve them? Do we want to teach our children to solve them?[43]

Given that I have emphasised the enormity of the problems we face in overcoming the bullying cycle, as well as the enormity of the burden placed on us as parents, it is well to heed Peck's challenging questions. We do teach our children, whether explicitly or implicitly, whether verbally or non-verbally. But what do we teach them? Is it to bemoan their trials and tribulations, to put themselves down for their failure to avoid suffering, to retaliate against unfair and cruel experiences, to loathe themselves? Or do we show them how to accept that life is difficult, that fear can be transcended by love, and that we can free ourselves to take on each difficulty as a challenge and opportunity for personal and social growth?

We may need to remind ourselves that our children are as likely as us to be caught up in all the roles of the bullying cycle. We are all a complex product of healthy and unhealthy relationships. Being parents of a particular social class, colour and religious background does not exempt us from the roles of the bullying cycle, nor does it inoculate our children against them. Life is difficult for all of us.

I mentioned earlier that it has been assumed that bullying is primarily a working-class and male issue. Stereotypical images of loud, rough, tough, unintelligent, coarse brutes, individually or in gangs, picking on timid, clever, respectable (and possibly bespectacled) innocents abound. Even current writers can get caught up in this belief. For example, with reference to the scope of extremist groups to recruit young members, it is claimed that 'poorer inner-city children with a tenuous sense of belonging are attracted to their distinctive policies of intolerance and their direct physical approach.'[44]

However, research has shown that children succeed in life, in social and emotional terms, if they have warm, caring and interested parents, and a home setting where they do not experience or witness bullying. This is far more important than socio-economic status. However, it is clear that the impact on parents due to the stress of low and inadequate incomes often indirectly affects the child – less significantly in material terms than in the emotional support parents can give and the amount of discord generated within the house as parents berate each other for the anxieties and pressures they are having to face.

Being poor is much more manageable for everyone where there is a strong sense of caring and support. There is no causal connection between material possessions or lack of them and the bullying cycle. It is the poverty of emotional experiences, as well as the experience of abuse by parents and other adults, that breeds and grooms young people to play their roles in the bullying cycle.

I want to consider the cases of Jon Venables and Bobby Thompson, the two ten-year-old boys who killed two-year-old James Bulger in Bootle in February 1993. I am grateful to David James Smith who, in his remarkable account of the murder (*The Sleep of Reason*), describes the different family backgrounds of Jon and Bobby.[45]

Jon's childhood experiences are somewhat unclear, but there is considerable evidence that his childhood was characterised by instability. There were parental separations and divorce, Jon living first with one parent, then another, the parents both being unable to cope at times and sending him to the other.

> [Jon's] increasingly disturbed behaviour is a clue to the feelings of confusion, insecurity and rejection aroused in him by this continuing upheaval and uncertainty. The violence and aggression he displayed at school and at home also suggest a build-up of frustration, resentment and anger.[46]

Smith continues by alluding to domestic conflict and makes an important assertion: 'Being a child witness to such conflict would be distressing enough. Being a victim of it. . . . could only have reinforced the impotent, powerless frustration of Jon's position'.[47]

Jon's parents had troubled upbringings themselves, the mother probably experiencing harsh physical punishment and criticism, the father losing his mother when young. Both suffered from depression, and the father is assessed as passive and incapable. Jon's father was aware of Jon being bullied and considered it 'just part of growing up'. Smith suggests that the father (to whom Jon was known to be hostile) is passing on his passive and vulnerable characteristics.

It seems to me that Jon's family provided an archetypal family environment in terms of role models whose beliefs and attitudes, thoughts, feelings and actions could not be better designed to induce and train Jon to play the roles of bully, victim and rescuer.

Moreover, at the point when Jon begins to unburden himself, in great distress, by admitting the murder, '[the parents] tell him, as they have been advised to do, that they will always love him. It is the trigger for the enormous emotional release of Jon's guilt.'[48]

Smith then poses two fundamental questions.

Is it possible that the potency of those words – the expression of 'love' – was not just a result of Jon's need to hear them, when the desire to confess had become overwhelming? Is it also possible that he had not heard them very often in the past and had doubted, or at least not always been sure of, his parents' love?[49]

Bobby's childhood was also ideally suited to produce bullies and victims.

Conflict and violence were an inbuilt part of life in the Thompson household. We probably don't know the half of what Bobby witnessed and was subjected to, but what we do know provides a vivid picture of a classically dysfunctional family.[50]

Bobby's mother had herself been terrorised by a drunk and physically abusive father, and unsupported by a passive mother. She feels unloved and worthless. She marries a man (Bobby's father) who had been brought up harshly by older brothers and who then within marriage became a drunken abuser. They have many children and there is little love expressed in the family. Violence and conflict abounds on all sides. The father eventually leaves, the mother adopts the role of victim and abuses alcohol. She is incapable of parenting, and in a repeat of the father's upbringing Bobby's older brothers are left to bring him up.

The experience of conflict and violence – the deliberate and unintentional abuse of adult power – is their only model. . . . We don't know what went on but, at best, it was probably bullying and, at worst, it may have reached into those dark corners of excessive abuse.[51]

Bobby was victim and bully. He was also rescuer to his mother, wanting to please and protect her, and it may well be that his resolve to protect her led to his aggressive and defiant resistance to the police during their interviews with him.

As I stated earlier (in Chapter 2), stealing and extortion are often not undertaken for material gain. Bobby went shoplifting, and then threw away what he had stolen. It is the element of self-loathing, the desire to be punished or punish oneself, that comes to the fore.

> He is self-destructive because he doesn't know any better and no one is there to make any sense of it for him. He has reserves of anger and resentment and unsatisfied needs. He has experienced abuse of power and will one day impose his own power to abuse.[52]

The combination of Jon and Bobby was no doubt a determining factor in their course of action in abducting and murdering James Bulger. However, like the case of Thomas Hamilton referred to earlier, it would have been impossible to predict that these two boys would have committed this act. Indeed, without understating the difficult childhoods of Venables, Thompson and Hamilton, many people of all ages may have had more traumatic experiences than these three.

What we do need to be aware of, therefore, is that there are considerable numbers of children and adults in the community who have the potential to commit such acts, and find other ways and opportunities to express their childhood disturbance and lack of love. They will abuse themselves in many ways: through bullying others, or being open to self-abuse, or to being abused by others.

The ultimate consequence of insecurity and despair is self-loathing. The ultimate consequence of self-loathing is violence to others and suicide. Hamilton did both. Violence and suicide are the endemic symptoms of a self-loathing society.

Not all childhood disturbance is rooted in physical abuse. In my career as a social worker there were numerous examples of children, from very poor to reasonably affluent homes, who were deprived of love, and had learnt to interpret the acquiescence of a parent to demands to hand over money as the gesture of affection. One girl constantly craved her father's care and attention, even a glimmer of interest. If she moaned enough, he would reach into his pocket and hand over some cash. He paid her to go away. Her reaction was to fritter and waste the money he had given her, as a re-expression of the devaluation she felt that his response had conveyed of her as a person.

Material possessions are always inadequate substitutes for love, whether they are given, stolen or extorted. Or whether they are given as tokens of pity. Or as tokens of shame. One of the most destructive and popular ways of responding to victims is to reward them with money. The greater the victimisation the greater the rewards, and the case of the Dunblane Massacre is one of many instances where the collective response has been one of pity and shame rather than compassion. I consider there is nothing compassionate or healthy or loving about giving huge amounts of money to parents whose children have been murdered. But I will focus here on the notion of tokens and deals.

As parents we may well consider that we give a good deal to our children. I have used that term deliberately, as it has two common meanings. First, it implies we give a lot; secondly, it implies that they come off better in the bargain – either better than us as parents, or better than we did as children, or better than children of other parents. We may wish to re-evaluate how good a deal we actually provide, and in particular question whether or not we are determining the bargain, a bargain that primarily meets our needs.

Perhaps we are doing deals explicitly, such as 'if you do this, I'll do this'. Most parents do this with their children from the time they are toddlers through to teenagers. It is an open contract, albeit generally from the position of parental power. It is frequently a deal more on our terms than our children's.

More often the deal is implicit rather than explicit. It may appear to be about giving but it is really about getting: 'look at how wonderful a parent I am, I want you to appreciate that, and give me the love I need'. Few parents can genuinely claim that from the point of conception onwards their child-rearing was not actually about meeting their own needs. This is not to say that we as parents neither care for our children nor attempt to meet their needs, but that it is unusual for it to be a one-way process.

The establishment in law of parental rights (which are extensive) over children's rights (which are minimal) enshrines the power of parents over their children. Power can corrupt, it can be abused. The extent of parental abuse of their children, whether physical, sexual and – most devastatingly – emotional, is terrifying and goes largely unrecorded until those children, retrospectively as adults, later disclose some of the torments they experienced. By that time they may be abusers themselves, or in abusive relationships with their partners and parents of their children.

Do we, can we, give unconditionally? If everything we give is part of an unspoken and unacknowledged deal, conscious or otherwise, based on our needs to get, then that is the message that will be received by our children. It is a message based on fear. For if the motivation behind giving is really about getting back, a destructive cycle is created.

> More likely the question will become 'am I getting enough?' This kind of thinking sets up an incredible need to control others so you won't feel short-changed, destroys your peace of mind and creates anger and resentment.[53]

Moreover, before we can offer the love and support to our children that they undoubtedly need, we have to establish how we get supports for ourselves, as explained in the previous chapter. Unfortunately, and paradoxically, the support we often seek is that of our children. If we depend on our children to support us, who is going to support them? Are we not training them how to rescue victims, to meet unfulfilled needs for love through meeting the needs of others?

I believe the work of both Maslow (on human needs) and Erikson (on human growth and stages of development) may be usefully considered here.

Maslow's hierarchy of human needs is reasonably well-known.[54] Although there are a number of other writers who have identified the needs of children and adults, Maslow encapsulates the essential elements of many of them and, usefully, places them in an order of ranking within a pyramid:

Figure 3. Maslow's hierarchy of human needs

5   Self-actualisation   5

4   Self-esteem   4

3 Love, Affection and Belonging 3

2   Safety Needs   2

1   Physiological or Survival Needs   1

The needs of a person have to be met at each stage from the base upwards. If the needs of a lower stage are unmet, then it will be impossible to effectively attain the next stage in the process of self-fulfilment. The stages are largely self-explanatory, but I will briefly elaborate their meaning.

Stage 1 represents the basic need for shelter, nourishment, warmth and adequate clothing. Within all societies, however civilised they may claim to be, there are substantial populations whose survival needs are frequently unmet in part.

Stage 2 represents the need for physical and emotional security. Being part of the bullying cycle would immediately put these needs in jeopardy. The enormity of the investment we have in perpetuating the bullying cycle helps explain why so many of us struggle to reach stage 3.

Stage 3 represents the needs to be loved, which includes being accepted, respected, and valued; and having a sense of belonging, and being able to enjoy positive friendships.

Stage 4 represents what Hastings has termed self-love, the elements of which are self-esteem, self-confidence, self-worth and self-respect.[55] To this stage I would add the need for self-discipline and self-control. We need to feel good about ourselves, to have positive self-belief, and receive positive recognition and attention, as well as praise, encouragement and appreciation.

Stage 5 represents our spiritual and creative potential to realise our true selves, to experiment and release our talents, to express and develop our beliefs and integrate them with our thoughts, feelings and actions.

Erikson introduced eight stages of human development (or 'eight ages of man' as he originally termed them).[56] The importance of these stages of development is, like Maslow's hierarchy of human needs, that they are cumulative – that is, if an earlier stage has not been reached and resolved healthily, it will impair the ability to cope appropriately with later stages until reparative work is undertaken.

Here is a short outline of some of the essential aspects of Erikson's eight ages/stages:

1. Basic Trust v. Basic Mistrust

Trust is two-fold. It requires an ability to be sure of the reliability of specific 'outer providers': that there are people who are there to help us meet our basic needs. We need to be able to trust others. But we also need to experience ourselves as trustworthy: that we can trust ourselves, and that those who provide for us do not need to be wary of us or on their guard.

2. Autonomy v. Shame and Doubt

From a basis of trust we need to be positively guided towards the autonomy of free choice. However, if we are denied this scope for autonomy or are dealt with by being shamed, we do not learn propriety or humility. Instead we turn our needs to discriminate against ourselves, becoming manipulative and acting secretively to 'get away' with things.

'From a sense of self-control without loss of self-esteem comes a lasting sense of good will and pride; from a sense of loss of self-control and of foreign overcontrol comes a lasting propensity for doubt and shame.'[57]

3. Initiative v. Guilt

Being able to plan and undertake tasks, to engage actively in doing something new, to have goals, are all part of using initiative. Initiative builds on the ability to trust oneself and be autonomous in choices. However, there is a danger in experiencing guilt in two ways: either over the goals that we have set ourselves and the tasks involved in achieving them, or through a sense of failure which in addition to guilt also induces resignation and anxiety.

4. Industry v. Inferiority

Industry, that ability and desire and readiness to work for oneself rather than rely primarily on being sustained by the providers, follows the development of initiative. We apply ourselves to the development of skills and the use of tools and equipment to achieve tasks. We see the world as something we can fashion.

However, there is a danger that we feel inadequate and inferior. We do not have faith in our abilities or our tools, or our position and status among our peers. We may feel different from and lesser than our peers.

'Many a child's development is disrupted when family life has failed to prepare him for school life, or when school fails to sustain the promises of earlier stages.'[58]

5. Identity v. Role Confusion

It is often considered that adolescence is a particularly troubled and troublesome time. While we must not neglect the importance of the earlier four stages, this stage presents a trial for growing and developing youths, who:

> . . . faced with this physiological revolution within them, and with tangible adult tasks ahead of them, are now primarily concerned with what they appear to be in the eyes of others as compared with what they feel they are, and with the question of how to connect the roles and skills cultivated earlier with the occupational prototypes of the day.[59]

The very real danger of this stage is role confusion: who and what and how should I be? Self-doubts and confusion about identity result in fear, a fear that can lead to the creation of tribes or clans of young people who bond together to reinforce their identity and who can ostracise and exclude those whom they portray as different, as outsiders. This behaviour is defensive, a destructive attempt to combat role confusion and uncertainty. This is often the basis for racial and sexual segregation, and the abuse of those who do not fall into the prescribed grouping. When an individual feels very vulnerable about his or her identity, there is comfort in bonding with others who can protect that vulnerability by projecting a strong image. However, there is often a confusion between what is strong and violent. Many political movements are founded on aggression.

6. Intimacy v. Isolation

The tension between identity and role confusion exposes the young adult to vulnerability, but:

> emerging from the search for and insistence on identity, is eager and willing to fuse his identity with that of others. He is ready for intimacy, that is, the capacity to commit himself to concrete affiliations and partnerships and to develop the ethical strength to abide by such commitments, even though they may call for significant sacrifices and compromises.[60]

The avoidance of intimacy as experienced through close friendships, physical, emotional and spiritual closeness, and sexual partnerships, can lead to isolation and the destruction of those people and 'forces' who are perceived as threats to our intimate being.

7. Generativity v. Stagnation

As children are dependent so are adults. Adults need to be needed, and the main way that this is experienced is by guiding the younger generation – as parents and teachers and priests. Stagnation is the preoccupation with self-concern. The fact that parents have children, whether or not they actually want them, does not presume this concept of generativity.

Indeed, the need to be needed can be inverted so that the child is expected to parent the adult.

8. Ego Integrity v. Despair

Ego integrity 'implies an emotional integration which permits participation by followership as well as acceptance of the responsibility of leadership'.[61] At this stage there is a deep sense of spirituality. This includes an acceptance of the life cycle, which acknowledges and does not fear death. Despair is the feeling that time is too short, even that all is lost. Erikson paraphrases the relationship between adult integrity and infantile trust as follows: 'healthy children will not fear life if their elders have integrity enough not to fear death'.[62]

Comparing and linking the models of Maslow and Erikson can be instructive. For example, it is possible to see how inadequate provision of basic needs, such as for physiological survival or safety, can lead to specific psychological difficulties in later life stages, eg. inability to trust, feeling shame and guilt, and so on. It is important for us to reflect on how well our needs and stages have been met, as well as how we help our children to meet their needs and progress healthily through their stages of development.

The bullying cycle is fed by people of all ages who have not had their needs met satisfactorily and who have not been able or helped and guided satisfactorily through their stages of development. Love is the basis for the progression through and fulfilment of these stages. Miller identifies four steps towards full adult development, which if unfulfilled will produce a child (and later an adult) who will be in conflict with self and others.[63] Her four steps are: 'being allowed to describe sensations; to experience and express emotions; to query a situation; and to articulate needs'.[64]

I have proposed below a different, but not unrelated, set of ways in which children need to experience love, which for me is the basis of their healthy development into full adulthood.

But first there are two steps for parents to take. The first step is to ensure that we as parents have had and still do have the necessary basis for support. We need to ensure our needs, including unfulfilled needs from childhood, have been adequately met.

The next step is for us to love our children. By 'our children' I mean all those who are entrusted to our care, and by 'love' I mean being freed up, physically and emotionally, to see, hear and understand our children, and commit ourselves to their physical, emotional, social, educational and spiritual growth. There are five main ways in which we can help to do this.

(a) Listening

We need to develop the ability and willingness to listen to what our children are saying, not only verbally but through their actions and other non-verbal communication. We listen through our ears, our eyes, our mind. Freeing ourselves up to listen means we do not prejudge or make assumptions about what they have to, or should, say. We are open to them. We convey that what they have to communicate is important, is worthwhile. They are worthwhile.

We communicate that we are open to listening to them express their beliefs, their thoughts, their feelings and their actions.

(b) Assessing and revising

We need to develop the ability and willingness to assess and revise our perceptions. Through listening to our children we may hear unfamiliar and uncomfortable things about them and about us. We need to show them how we can assess, revise and learn from our beliefs, our thoughts, our feelings and our actions. The ability to re-frame our understanding of people and events is a vital component in breaking the bullying cycle.

(c) Engaging

We need to develop our ability and willingness to spend time with our children, to engage with them in reflection on their beliefs about themselves and their world, to analyse issues that are important to them, to express and share feelings, and to review their actions. Engaging is not judging or negatively criticising. It is an exploration.

(d) Helping

We need to develop our ability and willingness to help our children. They are not to be rescued from their difficulties, but aided to survive and grow from their experiences, and find further opportunities to meet their needs and develop their potential.

It is painful to watch them struggle with their self-doubts and beliefs. To help them we are there for them. We do not tell them what to believe, or give simplistic reassurances. Nor do we leave them to flounder. We assure them of our presence, our support, our unconditional love.

Their thoughts may be jumbled and confused, or appear distorted and partial, but to help our children we do not tell them the answers. We give them markers and sources of information for them to explore, and the support and encouragement to do so.

Their feelings may be excruciating, but to help them we do not tell them they are wrong or getting things out of proportion. We do not humour them, nor do we take on their pain for them. We are beside them, truly with them as they express and relieve themselves of their feelings. We give witness to the fact that there are no wrong emotions, that they exist, are free from moral taint, and are able to be shared.

We need to help them with their behaviour, not by prohibiting or sanctioning, but by example and guidance. We help them by planning with them, not for them. We allow them to take risks and make mistakes, without setting them up to fail by neglecting to protect them from unnecessary dangers. We assist them in developing skills in their own way and of their choosing, by placing opportunities unconditionally for them.

(e) Bonding

We need to develop the ability and willingness to build a spiritual link with our children which is neither about ownership nor biology. We are entrusted with their care and upbringing, but not with the rights to their service. There is a mutual spiritual indebtedness as one human to another, as having shared a journey of deep personal growth with each other. Bonding is the basis of true compassion and empathy.

Exercises

The Parenting Skills.

We need encouragement and time to develop and learn the skills of: listening; assessing and revising; engaging; helping; bonding. We need opportunities and support to practise these skills.

I suggest a parenting skills diary may be a practical way to approach this, whereby you set times aside each day, first to prepare yourself to develop one of the skills, and secondly some other time during the day to practise it – whether with your children or children entrusted to your care, or with a partner or colleague.

I also suggest that you call upon the supporters you identified in the exercise at the end of Chapter 6 to help you with your practice. These supporters can give you constructive feedback on whether your listening skills, for example, are experienced in the way you intend them to be.

Case Examples

Issue 7: In loco parentis

If you were a teacher how would you set about developing and using the five skills identified in Chapter 7 – listening, assessing and revising, engaging, helping, bonding – with the young people in the examples?

Which young people would you choose to do this with?

Who would you seek support from to do this?

BULLYING, THE CHURCH AND THE COMMUNITY

Children are born innocent, both harmless and powerless. If they become confused and ignorant, violent and depraved, destructive and self-destructive, then the society that produces them must be so too.[65]

Violence is not a natural (and therefore excusable) tendency. Indeed, there is nothing inevitable about it at all. But violence is pervasive. Images of violence are witnessed by us and our children in many ways.

We are bystanders when we witness the portrayal of physical, sexual and emotional violence in the media of our communities. As bystanders we allow ourselves and our children to witness passively this violence. We allow our children to view the popular television media heroes as they model alternative roles to those we believe are healthy. We allow ourselves to witness these models and be influenced by them, dulled to the messages conveyed by them and the destruction caused by them.

Our televisions are alternative parents for our children. But what kinds of parents are they? Detached, indifferent, uncaring, impersonal, violent, intrusive, unlistening, seductive, aggressive. There is a built-in power imbalance, and the only redress allowed to the watchers is to exclude the message-givers. There is no dialogue with a television set, no participation.

The UNICEF Children's Charter, launched in 1991 and encapsulating the tenets of the UN Convention on the Rights of the Child earlier adopted in 1989, enshrines four simple but fundamental basic rights for all children. These are: the right of survival; the right of protection; the right of education; and the right of participation. In a survey of adults in Scotland, reported in August 1996, 84% of those responding supported the concept of participation. This suggests, at least at the levels of thinking and belief, that there is a groundswell of support for a new basis of adult-child relationships.

There was within the reaction to the reported survey some qualifications regarding the nature and limits of participation. There was some anxiety that either parents could interpret this as allowing or encouraging their children effectively to bring themselves up (an abdication of parental responsibility to ensure survival, protection and education); or to engender fear among parents that their children would usurp their rights. This suggests to me that, on the one hand, participation is seen as a 'good thing'; but, on the other hand, if it threatens us directly or indirectly. . . .

However, the principle of participation requires us neither to discard parental responsibility nor to replace all parental rights. It does, however, place the rights of children on no less a level than those of adults. It eschews an ethos of equality, in effect promoting a culture where all people are 'equal but different'. The basis of participation is through mutual and genuine respect for self and others. In the previous chapter I suggested five elements of this participation: listening; assessing and revising; engaging; helping; and bonding.

I also suggested that compassion and empathy were the basis of bonding. We are born with the ability to express our common humanity through bonding, through empathy. Empathy is the missing ingredient in each of the roles in the bullying cycle. By regaining our ability to empathise, we dissolve and resolve our differences, and find common cause. Yet we fear that by reaching out to others through empathy we lose something of ourselves.

The fears have not disappeared. Fear of participation – which may invoke fears of loss of control, of the unknown, of being exposed, of the weaknesses that will become apparent in us, of the dislike we have of ourselves for our behaviour, of being worthless and useless, of not mattering any more, of being disposable – is vying with the positive thoughts we may have about it. Participation implies love, a commitment to equality and respect, to the value of each of us as unique and important human beings. Yet again we see not only the potential power of love in overcoming and transcending fear, but the inhibitions we have in facing up to our fears. Yes, it's a good idea. But. . . .

Our feelings and beliefs can talk us out of change. I recall Mao Tse Tung being quoted, in translation, as postulating what I regard as two very important premises from which to build a community based on love. The first of these is: 'a good idea is not a good idea unless and until it is put into practice'. The second is: 'dogma is less useful than pig-dung'.

The hardest element of change for us as individuals (which is why we present our own greatest resistance to it) is that if we have not yet met our own needs beyond Stage 2 of Maslow's hierarchy, or have become stuck with guilt or inferiority or role confusion, as in Erikson's 'ages', then we are going to struggle to operate successfully on a level that is representative of a higher or later stage.

Chapter 5 showed how we could go about tackling some of the difficulties we may have in relating positively to ourselves and to other people, but the need for support, to find others who can help meet our needs and facilitate our change, was emphasised in Chapter 6. However, I do not believe that the scope for sustaining longer-term growth as individuals or as societies can be dependent on the majority of us locating and using the supports of some sort of élite among us who have attained elevated or later stages of human development.

Perhaps life is becoming more difficult or, to be accurate, more difficult for us as parents because we have lost our purpose and direction within a materially obsessed culture.

Pat Collings, a recently retired head teacher from Derby, expressed her concerns about the nature of our society and the abilities of parents.

> I do honestly believe we're becoming a crueller society, and that there's not much demonstration of love for children. Society doesn't say anything positive to them and parents seem to need more help than they used to in just the basic things. Maybe we need a course in how to manage yourself in this new age. How you think and feel and listen – the basic things that make you into the human being you are. [66]

It seems to me that there is an evident and eminent need to find a source of strength and support that is neither based solely on the success of individual techniques to promote relaxation, self-esteem and assertiveness, nor on the willingness and ability of others to meet our needs and give us unconditional love. This is not to say that these are unimportant – quite the opposite. They are vital for society to survive and thrive without us all destroying each other. But they are not enough.

We need to gain a purpose, a vision of what life is about, a spiritual awareness that will hold and sustain us through all the adversity, stress, confusion, distraction, destruction and pain that comprises life. We need to engage with others, to share that vision, to help each other bring that vision into being.

What are our visions? Do we have a dream which we wish to create of ourselves as parents? What can we do to prevent ourselves being rendered impotent, to avoid the pitfalls of complaints that we are incomplete or incompetent?

It seems to me that we have powerful structures, institutions and organisations within our world societies that are, in theory, eminently suited to the sharing of our visions and the promotion of mutual inter-dependence. Fundamentally we have our families, where our common bonds are generally strongest, and where our visions could receive the greatest nourishment and support. We have our schools and churches, and our community groups, clubs and commercial and leisure infrastructure. How potent these can be to engender and foster creativity. Then there are government bodies and departments, based on a collective vision and in existence to promote the common good, the fulfilment of us as individuals and social groups.

But how often is it really like that? How often is our invest-ment in all these structures, institutions and organisations used to control and suppress us, to destroy our self-esteem, our self-belief, our spirituality, our potential to develop as unique, creative, loving members of society? How often do we say 'no' to ourselves, our children, our relatives and friends, and our colleagues, rather than 'yes'? That 'yes' says we have a moral imperative to be all we can be, for the good of our-selves and our fellow human beings.

Some families, some schools, some organisations and some churches do have visions and ideals towards which they strive. They do have purpose, and they give us good examples. But it is no coincidence when these good examples then come under fire. There is no threat greater than that of a good example.

The institutions that have vision and purpose feel different. For example, it is no coincidence that schools, sometimes denominational schools but by no means exclusively so, that have an explicit set of values which are shared among the staff are more able to create an environment which promotes pos-itive relationships and are more open to addressing bullying in constructive ways.

There is a feeling I get when I enter these schools which cannot be ascribed to the state of the building or furnishings, the temperature, the first person I meet, or any other specific material factor. What I experience is an atmosphere, an over-powering sense that this school has a vision which is whole-some, which is more than caring, more than striving for success, more than accommodating.

It is the presence of a culture which has the capacity to value and respect each of its members, to welcome strangers, to promote the development of all the aspects of each individual (not just their intellectual or physical abilities); and the humility to forgive their failings. It is a culture based not on fear but on love, whatever the pain, whatever the effort; and it is a culture which has as its essence a true sense of spirituality.

If I could bottle that essence and sell it, I would be assisting in creating a world-wide force for human growth; and, should I be materially minded, I would make a fortune! So how do we go about getting that essence, if it doesn't come pre-packed in bottles?

In schools, as in any other organisation, there is a need first to establish a value system that promotes positive relationships. The value system is not a policy document, neatly typed and brought out when the school is inspected. It is a living, ever-present approach to life and work, encapsulated and articulated in the beliefs, thoughts, feelings and actions of each member of the school. The staff set the tone, they provide the role models, they give the lead.

It follows that there is a need to address the existence of the bullying cycle first within staff relationships. My first video package *Bully No More!* was specifically aimed at school staff – all school staff, not just teachers or managers. How staff prioritise time and energy to address relationship issues among themselves reflects to pupils how seriously or otherwise the school is concerned about bullying.

Likewise within families, there needs to be a shared understanding of why each person is there. Why did we choose our partners? How committed are we to them? How do we express our love for them? Have we ever really shared what we believe about ourselves, our lives together, our future?

Why did we choose to have children? How able and prepared are we to care for them and love them? How do we allow and encourage each of us to grow, develop, change? Most importantly, perhaps, how do we express our beliefs and feelings?

How do we allow and respond to conflict? Do we allow it at all? Or would we rather brush things under the carpet, pretend that all is well, or moan and complain, or feel sorry for ourselves?

Because we can choose how to live, we are responsible for our actions and inactions. But we also share a complicity, a collective responsibility for the lives of our families, communities and society. If the bullying cycle exists we must accept our complicity. Likewise, we cannot turn away from the death of Jesus and say it was nothing to do with us. The suffering continues.

The greatest challenge and no doubt the hardest task for any family, any school, any church, any group, club or organisation is to promote community. I have suggested elsewhere (Kevin Brown, *To Bully No More! The Pupil Pack* 1994) that a blown-up poster of the following extract, displayed strategically around a school where staff (and pupils) can mingle, discuss and reflect on it, could provide a potent starting-point. (The poster is relevant for all kinds of institutions, not just schools.)

> In genuine community there are no sides. It is not always easy, but by the time they reach community, members have learned how to give up cliques and factions. They have learned how to listen to each other and how not to reject each other.
>
> Sometimes consensus in community is reached with miraculous rapidity. But at other times it is arrived at only after lengthy struggle.
>
> Just because it is a safe place does not mean community is a place without conflict. It is, however, a place where conflict can be resolved without physical or emotional bloodshed and with wisdom as well as grace.
>
> A community is a group that can fight gracefully![67]

If I argued cogently in a book on self-help that allowing ourselves one hour's extra sleep a day kept us in excellent physical and mental health, I could envisage a significant fairly immediate take-up of this idea, with a slow falling-off thereafter as many people reverted to previous patterns of behaviour. Others, though, would never take up this new pattern. They would complain that they had insufficient time, others always made too many demands, or that they will start doing it when they've got past some particular obstacle. In effect, they are saying 'I am not wanting to be well'. Perhaps 'I am already too unwell'. Certainly 'I do not like myself enough to be well'.

I wonder at the response to this book. Some may say it is a good idea – but for other people. Effectively they, those unknown masses, are the ones who need to do something, they are the ones to blame anyway. Some may say they have too much on their plate just now – so we can't blame them can we? Some may consider it a threat, feel blamed and blameworthy, and discard it. Some may say that they would have been able to do something had I written it better or explained it more fully or simply, or given better examples, or been more explicit about what they should do – in effect blaming me for their failure to respond; and so on.

Some will resolve to do something. But then they will discover that they do not know where to start, or how to start, or exactly when to start. They will lack the internal strength and faith, and the external supports, to help them begin to change, and remain powerless.

There will be some who will, quietly and undramatically and uncomplainingly, be different because they have read and thought about and felt the issues raised in this book. They will examine their beliefs about themselves and the world. Quite possibly they will have begun to share the ideas – not my ideas but their ideas, the outcome of their engagement with the material in this book – with their partner or a few trusted friends. In many small ways they will live differently. To the rest of us they will feel different. It won't be their clothes or their house or their car or any other aspect of their material lifestyle. It will be the atmosphere they create. It will be the ethos and culture that emanates from them, tangible yet largely invisible.

They will accept responsibility for the society in which they live – not the blame, not the false accolades, but the responsibility to lead by example which is central to the Christian way of life.

They won't be able to bottle and sell the spirit of reconciliation that exudes from their presence, but they will – by their quiet example – be promoting it in a deeper way. They will effectively wear a badge, both a statement of fact and an injunction to others, a badge which reads 'bully no more'.

NOTES

1. Olweus, D., 'Aggressors and their victims: bullying at school', in an edited book (source unknown).
2. Tattum, D.P. and Lane, D.A., *Bullying in Schools* (Trentham Books: Stoke-on-Trent, 1989).
3. Department for Education, *Bullying – Don't Suffer in Silence. An Anti-bullying Pack for Schools* (London: HMSO, 1994).
4. McTaggart, M., 'Signposts on the road to Hell' in 'First Appointments', *Times Educational Supplement* (5 May 1995).
5. Mellor, A., *Which Way Now? A Progress Report on Action Against Bullying in Schools* (SCRE: Edinburgh, 1995).
6. *Ibid,* p7.
7. Byrne, B., *Bullying: A Community Approach* (Columba Press: Dublin, 1994).
8. Erikson, E.H., *Childhood and Society* (Pelican: Harmondsworth, 1975).
9. Brown, K., *Bully No More! An Inter-Agency, Whole School, Non-Punitive Approach to Bullying* (St Andrew's College of Education: Glasgow, 1993), p13.
10. Brown, K., *Bully Off!* (First and Best in Education: Peterborough,1996).
11. Brown, K., *Bully No More!* (St Andrew's College of Education: Glasgow, 1993).

12. Train, A.G., *The Bullying Problem. How to Deal with Difficult Children* (Souvenir Press (Educational and Academic): London, 1995), p69.

13. Niemöller, M., *Congressional Records* (14 October 1968), p31636.

14. Bentley, J., *Martin Niemöller* (Oxford University Press: Oxford, 1984).

15. Besag, V.E., *Bullies and Victims in Schools* (Open University Press: Milton Keynes, 1989).

16. Strathclyde Regional Council, *Promoting Positive Relationships (Bullyproofing Our Schools)* (SRC: Glasgow, 1994).

17. Brown, K., *Bully Off!* (First and Best in Education: Peterborough, 1996).

18. Brandon, D., *Zen in the Art of Healing* (Routledge and Kegan Paul: London, 1976), p102.

19. Jenkins, R., *The Cone Gatherers.* (Paul Harris Publishers: Edinburgh,1980), pp182-3.

20. Brandes, D. and Ginnis, P., *The Student-Centred School* (Simon and Schuster Education: Hemel Hempstead, 1990), p112.

21. Hauck, P., *How To Stand Up For Yourself* (Sheldon Press: London, 1983), p27.

22. *Ibid,* p28. Author's emphasis.

23. Brandes, D. and Ginnis, P., *op cit,* p64.

24. McTaggart, M., *op cit.*

25. Bernstein, B., *Class, Codes and Control vol 1. Theoretical Studies Towards a Sociology of Language* (Paladin: St Albans, 1973), p218. Author's emphasis.

26. Train, A. G., *op cit.* p2.

27. *Ibid.*

28. *Daily Record* (8 August 1996). Author's emphasis.

29. Hauck, P., *op cit,* p14.

30. Dickson, A., *A Woman In Your Own Right* (Quartet Books: London, 1982), p156.

31. *Ibid.*

32. Hare, B., *Be Assertive* (Optima: London, 1994), p132.

33. *Ibid.*
34. *Ibid,* p15.
35. *Ibid,* p25.
36. *Ibid,* pp26–7. Author's emphasis.
37. Miller, A., *The Drama of Being A Child* (Virago: London, 1995), p98.
38. Peck, M., *A World Waiting To Be Born* (Arrow Books: London, 1994), pp205–6.
39. Maines, B. and Robinson, G., *The No Blame Approach* (Lame Duck Publishing: Bristol, 1992).
40. Hare, B., *op cit*, p32–4.
41. Brown, K., *To Bully No More! The Pupil Pack* (St Andrew's College of Education: Glasgow, 1994).
42. Yancey, P., *Where Is God When It Hurts?* (Marshall Pickering: London, 1990).
43. Peck, M.S., *The Road Less Travelled: A New Psychology of Love, Traditional Values and Spiritual Growth* (Rider: London, 1987a) p15. Author's emphasis.
44. Train, A., *op cit*, p24.
45. Smith, D.J., *The Sleep of Reason* (Arrow Books: London, 1995).
46. *Ibid*, p234.
47. *Ibid*, p235.
48. *Ibid*, p234.
49. *Ibid*, p234.
50. *Ibid*, p237.
51. *Ibid*, p239.
52. *Ibid*, p240.
53. Jeffers, S., *Feel the Fear and Do It Anyway* (Arrow Books: London, 1991), pp170–1.
54. Gross, R.D., *Psychology – The Science of Mind and Behaviour*, second edition. (Hodder and Stoughton: London, 1992), p902.
55. Hastings, J., *You're Great* (Touchstone Publications: Haslemere, 1995).
56. Erikson, E., *Childhood and Society* (Pelican: Harmondsworth, 1975).

57. *Ibid*, p246.
58. *Ibid*, p252.
59. *Ibid*, p253.
60. *Ibid*, p255.
61. *Ibid*, p261.
62. *Ibid*, p261.
63. Miller, A., *Banished Knowledge: Facing Childhood Injuries* (Virago: London, 1990).
64. Miles, R., *The Children We Deserve* (Harper Collins: London, 1994) p258.
65. *Ibid*, p7.
66. Wilce, H., 'Odds Against Them' in *Times Educational Supplement 2* (15 November 1996).
67. Peck, M.S., *The Different Drum: Community Making and Peace* (Arrow Books: London, 1987b), p71.

BIBLIOGRAPHY

Bernstein, B., *Class, Codes and Control vol 1. Theoretical Studies Towards a Sociology of Language* (Paladin: St Albans, 1973).

Besag, V.E., *Bullies and Victims in Schools* (Open University Press: Milton Keynes, 1989).

Brandes, D. and Ginnis, P., *The Student-Centred School* (Simon and Schuster Education: Hemel Hempstead, 1990).

Brandon, D., *Zen in the Art of Healing* (Routledge and Kegan Paul: London, 1976).

Brown, K., *Bully No More! An Inter-Agency, Whole School, Non-Punitive Approach to Bullying* (video/booklet package) (St Andrew's College of Education: Glasgow, 1993.

Brown, K., *To Bully No More! The Pupil Pack. Classroom Material to Overcome the Bullying Cycle* (2-video/booklet/resource material package) (St Andrew's College of Education: Glasgow, 1994).

Brown, K., *MASS ATTACK* (First and Best in Education: Peterborough, 1995a).

Brown, K., *Bully No More! Creating the New Climate* (First and Best in Education: Peterborough, 1995b).

Brown, K. *Bully Off! Towards a Whole New Ball Game of Relationships in Schools.* (First and Best in Education: Peterborough, 1996).

Byrne, B., *Bullying: A Community Approach* (Columba Press: Dublin, 1994).

Department for Education. *Bullying – Don't Suffer in Silence*: *An Anti-Bullying Pack for Schools* (London: HMSO, 1994).

Dickson, A., *A Woman In Your Own Right* (Quartet Books: London, 1982).

Elliott, M., *Keeping Safe. A Practical Guide to Talking with Children* (Coronet Books: London, 1994).

Gross, R.D., *Psychology – The Science of Mind and Behaviour*, second edition, (Hodder and Stoughton: London, 1992).

Hare, B., *Be Assertive* (Optima: London, 1994).

Jeffers, S., *Feel the Fear and Do It Anyway* (Arrow Books: London, 1991).

Jenkins, R., *The Cone Gatherers* (Paul Harris Publishers: Edinburgh, 1980).

La Fontaine, J., *Bullying: A Child's View* (Calouste Gulbenkian Foundation: London, 1991).

Maslow, A., *Motivation and Personality*, second edition, (Harper and Row: New York, 1970).

Mellor, A., *Which Way Now? A Progress Report on Action Against Bullying in Schools* (SCRE: Edinburgh, 1995).

Miles, R., *The Children We Deserve* (Harper Collins: London, 1994).

Miller, A., *Banished Knowledge: Facing Childhood Injuries* (Virago: London, 1990).

Miller, A., *The Drama of Being a Child* (Virago: London, 1995).

Olweus, D., *Bullying at School – What We Know and What We Can Do* (Blackwell: Oxford, 1993).

Peck, M.S., *The Road Less Travelled: A New Psychology of Love, Traditional Values and Spiritual Growth* (Rider: London, 1987a).

Peck, M.S., *The Different Drum: Community Making and Peace* (Arrow Books: London, 1987b).

Peck, M.S., *A World Waiting To Be Born* (Arrow Books: London, 1994).

Smith, D.J., *The Sleep of Reason* (Arrow Books: London, 1995).

Stewart, I., and Joines, V. *TA Today. A New Introduction to Transactional Analysis* (Lifespace Publishing. Nottingham, 1993).

Strathclyde Regional Council, *Promoting Positive Relationships (Bullyproofing Our Schools)* (SRC: Glasgow, 1994).

Tattum, D.P. and Lane, D.A., *Bullying in Schools* (Trentham Books: Stoke-on-Trent, 1989).

Train, A.G., *The Bullying Problem. How to Deal with Difficult Children* (Souvenir Press [Educational and Academic] Ltd: London, 1995).